HOT LINKS: THE GUIDE TO LINKING COMPUTERS

Hot Links

About the Enclosed Software

Disk Contents   All of the utilities on this disk are supplied by Traveling Software, Inc., and are copyrighted by Traveling Software, Inc.

The disk contains the superb LapWrite program. This text processor optimizes your disk space and even allows you to use expanded type (a great help if you are using a laptop). Also included is File Manager, a desktop utility to help you manage your files and directories. It is particularly effective when used with Desk Connect. There are two Desk Connect programs on the disk. Desk Connect allows you to exchange files using only a cable and the software in this book. You can use Desk Connect on a stand-alone PC or on a network. For more details see Appendixes A, B, C, and D of this book.

System Requirements   This software requires IBM PC or compatible Intel 8086 machines or higher, MS-DOS 3.1 or higher, and 640K of memory with at least 250K of disk space. To use Desk Connect, each PC must have one RS-232 serial or one parallel port. You also need one 9-pin or 25-pin serial connector cable or a 25-pin parallel connector cable, available from Traveling Software at its toll-free order line, 1-800-343-8080.

DISK WARRANTY

This software is protected by both United States copyright law and international copyright treaty provision. You must treat this software just like a book, except that you may copy it into a computer to be used and you may make archival copies of the software for the sole purpose of backing up our software and protecting your investment from loss.

By saying, "just like a book," Osborne **McGraw-Hill** means, for example, that this software may be used by any number of people and may be freely moved from one computer location to another, so long as there is no possibility of its being used at one location or on one computer while it is being used at another. Just as a book cannot be read by two different people in two different places at the same time, neither can the software be used by two different people in two different places at the same time (unless Osborne's copyright is being violated).

LIMITED WARRANTY

Osborne **McGraw-Hill** warrants the physical diskette(s) enclosed herein to be free of defects in materials and workmanship for a period of 60 days from the purchase date. If Osborne **McGraw-Hill** receives written notification within the warranty period of defects in materials or workmanship, and such notification is determined by Osborne **McGraw-Hill** to be correct, Osborne **McGraw-Hill** will replace the defective diskette(s).

The entire and exclusive liability and remedy for breach of this Limited Warranty shall be limited to replacement of defective diskettes(s) and shall not include or extend to any claim for or right to cover any other damages, including but not limited to, loss of profit, data, or use of the software, or special, incidental, or consequential damages or other similar claims, even if Osborne **McGraw-Hill** has been specifically advised of the possibility of such damages. In no event will Osborne **McGraw-Hill**'s liability for any damages to you or any other person ever exceed the lower of the suggested list price or actual price paid for the license to use the software, regardless of any form of the claim.

OSBORNE, A DIVISION OF McGRAW-HILL, INC., SPECIFICALLY DISCLAIMS ALL OTHER WARRANTIES, EXPRESS OR IMPLIED, INCLUDING BUT NOT LIMITED TO, ANY IMPLIED WARRANTY OF MERCHANTABILITY OR FITNESS FOR A PARTICULAR PURPOSE. Specifically, Osborne **McGraw-Hill** makes no representation or warranty that the software is fit for any particular purpose, and any implied warranty of merchantability is limited to the 60-day duration of the Limited Warranty covering the physical diskette(s) only (and not the software) and is otherwise expressly and specifically disclaimed.

This limited warranty gives you specific legal rights; you may have others that may vary from state to state. Some states do not allow the exclusion of incidental or consequential damages or the limitation on how long an implied warranty lasts, so some of the above may not apply to you.

HOT LINKS:
THE GUIDE TO
LINKING COMPUTERS

Mark Eppley
and
David Hakala

Osborne **McGraw-Hill**

Berkeley New York St. Louis San Francisco
Auckland Bogotá Hamburg London Madrid
Mexico City Milan Montreal New Delhi Panama City
Paris São Paulo Singapore Sydney
Tokyo Toronto

Osborne **McGraw-Hill**
2600 Tenth Street
Berkeley, California 94710
U.S.A.

For information on translations or book distributors outside of the
U.S.A., please write to Osborne **McGraw-Hill** at the above address.

Hot Links: The Guide to Linking Computers

1234567890 DOC 998765432

ISBN 0-07-881020-5

Publisher
Kenna S. Wood

Acquisitions Editor
William Pollock

Associate Editor
Vicki Van Ausdall

Technical Editor
Chuck Guzis

Project Editors
Linda Medoff
Paul Medoff

Copy Editor
Paul Medoff

Proofreader
Linda Medoff

Indexers
Phil Roberts
Peggy Bieber-Roberts

Computer Designer
Jani Beckwith

Illustrators
Susie C. Kim
Marla J. Shelasky

Cover Designer
Mason Fong

CONTENTS

ACKNOWLEDGMENTS

As with anything of this magnitude, this book is certainly not the product of just one individual. In fact, the credit for *Hot Links: The Guide to Linking Computers* should go to the many highly dedicated people who persevered through the ups and downs of its development and who kept on course, despite my best efforts to sidetrack them!

I've tried to acknowledge everyone who worked together on this project below. If I have missed someone, my sincere apologies.

To Marilyn, Michael, and Ann-Marie who are certainly more inspiration than one could ever deserve . . . and who always seem to open my eyes to linking issues that I tend to forget in the rush of day-to-day life.

To Dave Hakala, who constantly amazes me with his writing skill and technical knowledge. To Charlie Bermant, who is one of the few people I know who has been published in *Rolling Stone* and must be given the credit for getting this "book thing" off the ground. In fact, I doubt if you would be reading this book today if it weren't for Charlie.

Matt (Mr. Bothell) Bogusz relentlessly kept the focus on the subtle and not so subtle issues of Hot Links' content. Leo (the Leomeister) Manson did an outstanding job of creating all the great coupon deals in this book, together with Carmen (cc) Carbone. To Peter (Mr. Wireless) Rysavy who was instrumental in making sure that the latest "anti-cable" technologies were presented. Lyn Pawley and Nancy Ricci provided constant support and all the empty Fed Ex envelopes I needed. And to Mike (Mr. Modem) Begeman and Jon (The QAman) Holz.

John (Mr. BBS) Hedtke did a great job on the New Linking Challenges chapter and with multitasking the many threads of my conversation late one afternoon. And thanks to Sharon (JellyFish) Dunkel, who wrote the Desk Connect instructions.

Thanks to the many dedicated people at Osborne McGraw-Hill who worked nonstop to get this book out on time. Thanks to Mr. Bill (he doesn't work at Microsoft) Pollock, Jeff Pepper, Vicki Van Ausdall, Cindy Brown, Paul Medoff, and Linda Medoff, all of whom ensured that this book did not compromise on quality, while at the same time making the publishing schedule.

And last, but certainly not least, I would like to thank my parents whose initial linking efforts were responsible for inventing me. You taught me that one should not always follow the standard protocols in breaking through those ever-present communication barriers.

—Mark Eppley

A book on such a wide-ranging topic could not be written without the contributions and support of many fine people whose names do not appear on the cover. Special thanks are due to:

✦ Charles Bermant, who originally conceived the idea for this book, recruited the team, and researched much of its contents

✦ Bill Pollock and Jeff Pepper, two of the kindest and gentlest editors in the business

✦ John Hedtke, a busy author who found time to contribute his knowledge of pen-based and palmtop connections to Chapter 10

✦ Posey Gering of Attachmate Corp., who clued us in on PC-to-mainframe links

  Vicki Van Ausdall, Judy Kleppe, Paul Medoff, and the rest of the editorial and production team at Osborne McGraw-Hill, for pulling all the chapters together, even when they (always) arrived late.

—Dave Hakala

PREFACE

Welcome to Hot Links!

Whether this is your first "computer" book purchase, or you already own a number of computer books or software, I think you'll find the value of Hot Links and its software to be much more than you are expecting. You'll even find some great coupon deals (exclusive to this book!) on cables and Traveling Software, Inc., linking software products that will save you some big $$$ in your quest for linking.

I can't count the number of times that I've been asked at computer user group meetings and industry trade shows and forums, "Eppley, why don't you write a book about linking? I spent three hours trying to figure out what you just told me in three minutes. It would be great if I had one source to turn to to solve my day-to-day connectivity challenges."

This book is not an encyclopedia of connectivity. If it were, you would need a shopping cart to help you get it from the store shelf to your car.

What this book *will* do is provide you with some solutions and specific ideas for desktop PCs, laptop/notebook computers, Macs, and palmtop PCs and hand-held organizers. We've gone to extremes to make sure the appropriate depth of information is presented in a concise, well-organized manner so you don't have to spend a lot of effort wading through a bunch of fluff to get an answer to a specific linking question.

We also give you a glimpse of what I believe will be some of the products and technologies that will affect how and what we will be linking to in the near future. I think we are on the verge of a major technological and cultural shift in not only the kind of information we link to, but also the methods, tools, and information highways we will use to link.

I'm sure that nobody has yet to imagine what the future of linking will bring. But while I'm waiting for my imagination to get going, you'd do well to check out the real, practical linking tips on the pages ahead.

—Mark Eppley

INTRODUCTION

The goal of this book is to help you find the most cost-effective and easily implemented solution to your computer-linking needs. The chapters are arranged so that common and inexpensive solutions are first, and specialized or costly solutions come later.

Chapter 1 covers the fundamentals of parallel and serial communications. If you link even one printer to one computer, you need to know about parallel and serial ports, connectors, gender changers, and cables.

Chapter 2 applies parallel and serial links to the problem of sharing costly printers and other peripheral devices among groups of computers.

Chapter 3 discusses how to move files from one PC to another over parallel and serial cables. 95 percent of office linking needs can be met with these two solutions.

Chapter 4 provides an overview of local area networks, for people who need simultaneous access to data files. Three types of LANs—zero-slot, peer-to-peer, and client/server—offer progressively greater capabilities at higher cost.

Chapter 5 examines modems, terminal software, remote-control software, and electronic bulletin board systems. Modems extend your

linking options beyond the walls of home or office to any corner of the planet.

Chapter 6 is for laptop and notebook computer owners. It covers pocket modems and LAN adapters, how to put your portable to work at home with disk-sharing software, and how to replace your deskbound PC entirely, using laptops and docking stations.

Chapters 7 and 8 address ways of linking IBM-compatible PCs to Macintosh and mainframe computers, and translating files generated by one software program into formats another can use.

Chapter 9 covers a number of wireless linking methods. As companies reorganize, computers are often moved around in house; eliminating the need for cables is like putting wheels on desks that were formerly bolted to the floor. Traveling computerists will be interested in cellular-phone modems and packet-radio networks.

Chapter 10 examines palmtop and pen-based computers, and the so-called Personal Digital Assistants such as Sharp's Wizard, from a linking standpoint.

Appendix A discusses installation of the Hot Links software bundled with this book.

Appendix B discusses Desk Connect, the file-exchange software.

Appendix C discusses File Manager, the file-management program.

Appendix D discusses LapWrite, the word processor.

Appendix E provides names, addresses, and phone numbers of firms mentioned in each chapter, and others offering linking solutions.

Hot Links covers a very wide spectrum of linking topics. You will find yourself referring to this book many times over the years as your computing ambitions and requirements expand.

1

BASIC LINKING KNOWHOW: PARALLEL AND SERIAL COMMUNICATIONS

This chapter discusses the two most commonly used linking methods. Parallel and serial communications are found in every PC, from the movement of data between disk drives and main memory to the link between your PC and printer. The first three chapters of this book deal almost exclusively with parallel and serial links, so you should find yourself referring to this chapter quite often.

This chapter is a quick introduction to data communication techniques, and a novice's guide to hardware used for linking. Topics include the following:

✦ How data is stored and moved

✦ Parallel and serial links

✦ Synchronous and asynchronous serial communications

✦ Communications settings (data bits, parity, stop bits)

✦ Identifying the ports on your PC

✦ UARTs for high-speed linking

✦ COM ports, IRQs, and how to configure them to avoid conflicts

How Data Is Stored: Bits and Bytes

Computers perform all their complex functions by combining and manipulating millions of *bits*—short for *Binary digITs*. "Binary" means "made up of two parts," in this case the numbers 1 and 0. Bits are particularly well suited to computing because a bit can be represented by switching an electric current on (for 1) or off (for 0), something computers are very good and fast at doing. Everything a computer does is accomplished by combining and recombining these two elementary numbers.

Bits can be stored in many different ways. A 1 can be represented by a hole punched in a paper tape, while a 0 might be the absence of a hole. CD-ROM disks use lasers to burn a tiny pit in a metal disk to represent a 1, while the absence of a pit represents a 0. A piece of metallic film can be magnetized in one tiny spot. If the north magnetic pole is pointing in one direction, the spot represents a 1; if the north pole points in the opposite direction, the spot represents a 0. These are all ways to store bits in one place.

A single bit doesn't tell you much, but a group of bits read as a pattern can contain any amount of information, just as the 26 letters of the alphabet can form words, sentences, novels, or the Unabridged Oxford English Dictionary.

A group of bits is called a *byte* (pronounced "bite"). Bytes can theoretically be any number of bits in length, but computer designers generally work in powers of 2: 4, 8, 16, 32, 64, and so on.

How Bits Travel

A piece of paper (or a hard disk) is fine for storing stationary patterns of bits and bytes, but to move bits from one place to another requires a medium that moves. Electricity, comprised as it is of a moving stream of electrons, serves the purpose very nicely. All you have to do is alter the condition of one part of the electron stream in a certain way to represent a 1, and set the next part of the electron stream to another condition to represent a 0. As the electrons flow through a wire, the bits represented by each part of the stream are carried along like waves on a stream of water.

When a wave comes downstream, its crest is high relative to the water's normal level, and its trough is relatively low. A stream of water could be used to carry bits, with the crests of waves representing 1's and the troughs representing 0's. You can tell a crest from a trough simply by measuring the height of the water at any point and comparing it to the normal water level. When the water level is higher than normal, a 1 is "passing through." When the level is lower than normal, a 0 is passing through.

The voltage an electric current carries is a very easy condition to alter. For the purpose of visualizing how bits are represented, think of voltage as the height of a wave moving along a stream of water. The normal level of the water at rest is equivalent to the voltage the wire carries when the computer is doing nothing to it. This normal voltage level is called the *signal ground*.

When your computer needs to move a bit from one place to another (say, from a magnetized spot on a disk to a spot on your monitor), it first reads the original bit to determine if a 1 or a 0 is to be moved. Then the computer momentarily alters the wire's voltage above or below the signal ground level.

Figure 1-1 shows how the voltage on the wire varies over time. The signal ground voltage is labeled "0 volts" because it represents the base value from which the 1-bit and 0-bit voltages are measured. It makes no difference in this illustration whether the signal ground is 5 volts or 500 volts, or whether a 1 bit is 10 volts or 1000 volts higher than the signal ground. The important thing is the relative values of the voltages.

Figure 1-1 shows time along the horizontal axis and voltage along the vertical axis. One unit of time is the distance from A to B along the horizontal axis. The change from signal ground voltage to 5 volts above signal ground (+5v for short) begins at the point in time labeled A and continues for one time unit, to point B. This period of +5v on the wire represents a 1 bit.

It is easy to detect the moment at which a 0 bit follows the first 1 bit—the voltage drops to –5v at point B in time. You can also clearly tell that another 1 bit has been sent at point C in time, because the voltage again changes to +5v.

But what is happening between point C and point E in time; are we looking at two 1 bits sent back to back? Did the sending computer turn

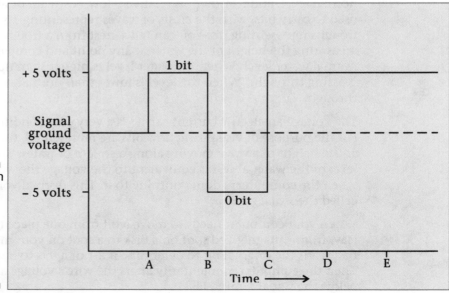

Timing diagram showing how voltage of a data wire changes over time

Figure 1-1.

the voltage up to +5v and just leave it there when it had no more bits to send? You can see that the receiving computer has a problem when two bits of the same kind are sent back to back.

Parallel Data Links

The sending computer needs to tell the receiver whether the +5v on the wire during the time interval D to E is a 1 bit that should be "counted" or just an idle signal that should be ignored.

One way to distinguish between bits and "dead air" would be to set the voltage back to the signal ground level in between every pair of bits, or at least between two bits of the same type. But that would insert useless space in the data stream. It would take much more time to transmit the same number of bits.

Another method uses a second wire running parallel to the wire that carries data bits. This second wire—called a *strobe wire*—tells the receiver what to do with the voltage on the data wire. When the strobe wire carries a 0 bit, the data wire's voltage should be ignored. When the strobe wire carries a 1 bit, the voltage on the data wire should be treated as incoming data.

The upper graph in Figure 1-2 shows the same time diagram of the voltage on the data wire that Figure 1-1 did. The lower graph shows a time diagram for a strobe wire running in parallel with the data wire. Three bits—a 1, a 0, and another 1—are sent along the data wire during the time interval A to D. The strobe wire's voltage remains at +5v during the whole interval A to D, telling the receiver to "pay attention" to the voltage on the data wire.

The sending computer flips the strobe wire's voltage to –5v at point D in time. This 0 bit on the strobe wire tells the receiver to ignore the data wire's voltage, even though it is still set to represent a 1 bit. When the sending computer wants to transmit another 1 bit (beginning at point E in time), it flips the strobe wire's voltage to +5v again, telling the receiver, "Pay attention to the data wire's voltage again."

With the strobe wire's help, it is clear that the +5v on the data wire from time C to time G is not a single 1 bit or a series of four 1 bits. *Three* 1 bits are sent during the interval C to G, with one period of "idle time," D to E.

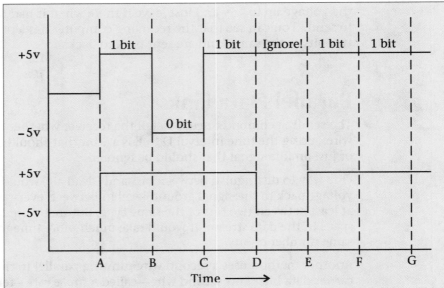

The strobe wire tells the computer when to ignore the data wire
Figure 1-2.

The beauty of this arrangement is that one strobe wire can serve any number of data wires, not just one as shown in this admittedly inefficient example. Strobe and data wires can be run from sender to receiver side by side; hence the term *parallel data communications* for this method of moving bits. Parallel links are fast, because several bits are moved during a given interval of time.

Your computer uses parallel links a lot inside its chassis. The flat ribbon cables connecting disk drives and printer ports to your motherboard are parallel links. The dozens of parallel bright metal tracks on the motherboard—the big circuit board that generally covers the entire bottom of a computer's case—are parallel links between one part of the computer and others. When people talk about the "16-bit bus" of an 80286 computer, or the "32-bit bus" of an 80386 machine, they are referring to parallel links that allow these machines to simultaneously move and manipulate 16 or 32 bits at a time.

Distance Limitations of Parallel Links

A parallel link moves data fast, but not very far. Ordinary parallel connections can be only 20 to 25 feet long. Custom cables and driver software can stretch a parallel connection up to 200 to 300 feet, but that kind of range is very expensive. Three problems limit the range of parallel links.

Skew is the tendency for the voltage waves on parallel wires to get out of synch with each other. There are always differences in physical and electrical characteristics between the wires that comprise a parallel cable. These differences effectively cause the waves of voltage on some wire(s) to fall behind those on others. Over short distances, the effect of skew is too small to matter. But over long distances, the 0 bit on the strobe wire might arrive at the receiving end before a data bit, causing the receiver to ignore that bit.

A second problem is *crosstalk.* Wires carrying electrical current generate magnetic fields. Magnetic fields can induce electric currents in other nearby wires. Over long distances, the closely bundled wires in a parallel cable tend to interfere with each other's signals.

A third problem, *electromagnetic radiation,* can extend far beyond the parallel cable and the wires in it. A lot of power is required to drive a signal over long distances; that's why long-distance electric transmission lines carry hundreds of thousands of volts instead of the 110-220 volts inside your home. The more power a cable carries, the wider its field of electromagnetic radiation; this field can extend dozens or hundreds of feet beyond the cable's electrical insulation. The FCC (Federal Communications Commission) regulates the amount of radiation various devices can emit, to minimize interference with television, air traffic control signals, and other vital communications. These regulations, plus the increasing power requirements, effectively limit the range of parallel links.

Serial Data Links

There is a reliable and inexpensive alternative to parallel links for long distances, though it is considerably slower. *Serial data communication* links use just one wire to transmit one bit at a time. Since there is no strobe wire, another method is used to determine when each bit starts and stops.

Synchronous Serial Links

The simplest serial communication depends on rigid synchronization at both ends. When sender and receiver first connect over the serial link, they agree upon the rate at which bits will be sent. This is commonly and erroneously called the *baud rate*; the accurate unit of measurement is *bits per second,* abbreviated *bps.* The sending and receiving computers rely on their internal clocks to measure the *bit interval,* the amount of time each bit should last.

Return to Figure 1-1 for a moment, and assume that the time interval represented by the space from A to B is 1/2400 second. If we assume bits are sent nose to tail, with no time between bits, then we are transmitting data at the rate of 2400 bps; the bit time is 1/2400 second.

So for 2400 bps communication, the sending computer sets the data wire's voltage to +5v when it wants to send a 1 bit, and waits exactly 1/2400 of a second (one bit interval) before sending another bit. If the second bit sent is a 0 bit, the voltage is flipped to –5v for the second bit interval (B to C in Figure 1-1). If the second bit is also a 1 bit, the sender just leaves the voltage at +5v for another bit interval.

The receiver keeps track of the voltage on the data wire *and* the number of bit intervals that pass. If the voltage remains +5v for three bit intervals, the receiver assumes three 1 bits have been sent back to back.

This type of *synchronous data communication* seems simple and efficient; only one wire is required, and you don't need to add any spaces between bits. But three questions must be addressed:

1. How does the sender tell the receiver when to start timing bit intervals and treating voltage as data?

2. If the sender must pause in its transmission of bits, how can it tell the receiver to temporarily stop treating voltage as data?

3. How does the sender tell the receiver that it is finished sending data bits?

All three questions are answered in the same fashion. After negotiating the bit interval with the receiver, the sender transmits a special pattern of bits that say, in effect, "Begin timing bit intervals and receiving data when this block of bits ends." The receiver treats everything after this start block as incoming data bits.

If the sender must pause for a while, it sends another special pattern of bits which, to the receiver, means "pause." The sender continues sending this bit pattern (called an *IDLE sequence*) until it is ready to resume transmitting data. The receiver discards the bits of each IDLE sequence; it does not pass them on to the computer as data.

Yet another bit pattern tells the receiver "OK, data transmission is over for this session." The receiver stops timing bit intervals and "listening" for data bits.

The start, pause, and stop bit patterns are defined in various protocols—sets of rules—used in serial communications. These protocols are similar to the way we humans communicate during a telephone conversation: "Hello!", "Hold on a second. . .," "Goodbye!"

Asynchronous Data Links

Synchronous serial communication is very efficient for sending large amounts of data in one direction at a time, with few pauses. But synchronous protocols are unsatisfactory for interactive communications sessions, such as a person searching an online database. Interactive sessions start, pause, and stop at irregular intervals, often after sending just one character in either direction. Synchronous protocols require that each block of data, no matter how long or short it is, be sandwiched between a start pattern and a stop bit pattern. In an interactive, character-at-a-time session, this packaging material would consume more time than the transmission of the useful data it frames. During pauses, the sender and receiver must transmit and track IDLE sequences to keep their clocks synchronized.

Asynchronous communication ("async" for short) solves these problems by dividing a stream of bits into *characters* of eight bits each, and clearly marking the beginning and end of each character. Async, like synchronous communications, relies on a negotiated bit interval to tell when each bit in a character starts and stops. But async adds a *start bit* at the beginning of each character and a *stop bit* at the end of each character. The start bit is always a 0, and the stop bit is always a 1.

Figure 1-3 shows the timing graph of an async character containing one start bit (always a 0), eight data bits (11010010 in this example), and one stop bit (always a 1), for a total of ten bit intervals.

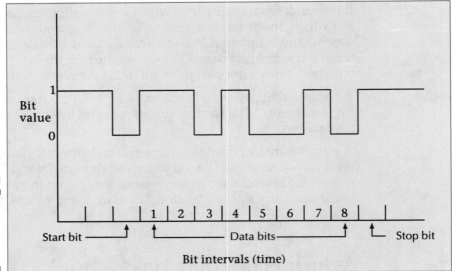

Timing diagram
of an
asynchronous
character
Figure 1-3.

Notice that there will *always* be a change from 1 to 0 between
characters because every character ends with 1, while the next one
always begins with 0. The receiver looks for such a change every ten bit
intervals. If the bit remains 1, the receiver knows no new character has
yet been sent. It stops counting bit intervals. When the bit flips to 0,
the receiver knows a new character is starting to come through, and it
starts counting bit intervals again.

The benefit of async communication is that the sending computer can
stop sending bits after one character and do something else for a while.
The receiver will patiently wait until it receives another start bit.

The drawback is less useful data transmitted per second. A synchronous
link would carry ten data bits in ten-bit intervals, while the async
character in Figure 1-3 carries only eight data bits in ten-bit intervals.
Thus, a 2400 bps synchronous link could carry 2400 data bits per
second, while an async link running at the same rate could only carry
(8 divided by 10 times 2400 =) 1920 data bits per second; the other 480
bits would be start and stop bits.

Parity: Who Needs It?

An asynchronous character doesn't have to be eight bits long. It can be any length the sender and receiver agree upon. Because the ASCII character set requires only seven bits to define all 128 characters, seven bits between start and stop bits are enough to transmit text.

Sending seven bits instead of eight would result in a ten percent gain in data throughput. It would take nine bits, including start and stop bits, instead of ten to send a character; $(10 - 9) / 10 = 0.10$ or ten percent less time to transmit one character.

But programmers are used to thinking in terms of eight-bit bytes used to store data; they found a use for the "extra" bit. It was put to work trying to detect errors that crop up in data during transmission over great distances.

The eighth bit was used to guarantee that each data character is of odd or even *parity*, depending on which type of parity the sender and receiver have agreed to use. Parity is the total count of all the 1 bits in a character.

The ASCII decimal code for the letter A, for instance, can be expressed as the bit pattern 1000001; this pattern contains two 1's, so its parity is 2. The letter C is equivalent to 1000011; its parity is 3, the number of 1's in its bit pattern.

Note that only seven bits are used to represent these text characters. If the sender and receiver use even parity to check for errors, all the characters sent must have even parity. So the eighth bit in a character is set to 0 if the character's seven-bit parity is already even, as it is with the letter A. But the eighth bit would be set to 1 for the letter C in order to make the eight-bit parity come out even.

When a character is received, its parity is recalculated. If there were no errors in transmission, the parity should be even if the sender and receiver agreed to use even parity error-checking. If the parity is as expected, the eighth bit is stripped before the data is passed on to its destination. If the parity is wrong, the receiver signals the sender to retransmit the character until it arrives with the right parity.

Parity checking achieved such popularity that the American National Standards Institute (ANSI) made it a standard for serial communication of text. Everyone wrote parity checking into their communications programs.

Then mathematicians discovered that parity checking does a very poor job of detecting the types of errors that occur in serial data transmission. However, it was too late to change the way thousands of programs worked and not worth the trouble anyway, since other error-correction methods had been added to serial communication.

So the flawed but harmless ANSI standard of seven data bits and even parity remains with us today. In PC-to-PC async communications, programmers make use of all eight bits to carry data. The common specification of "8-N-1" means eight data bits, no parity checking, and one stop bit. PC users usually encounter "7-E-1" (seven bits, even parity, one stop bit) communications settings only when they link to mainframes or when using mainframe-driven online services like CompuServe.

Ports You Plug Into

Your PC comes with a variety of *ports*: connectors into which you can plug peripherals and cables. Normally, you will find all the ports on the back side of your PC. The parallel and serial ports are used for general linking; others are designed for specific peripherals like keyboards, monitors, and mice. The task here is to identify the ports useful for linking.

Figure 1-4 illustrates the parallel and serial ports found on most PCs. Notice that their edges form trapezoids, four-sided shapes in which the two long sides are of unequal length. This shape makes it impossible to plug in a connector upside down; it will only go into the port one way.

Notice that some ports have pins (plugs) sticking out, while others have holes (sockets) going in. Ports showing plugs to the world are called *male,* while ports showing sockets are referred to as *female.*

Parallel ports are almost always female, while serial ports are generally male. Note that these are the standard genders of ports found *on your PC.* The cable connectors will have to be of the opposite gender.

Parallel ports almost always have 25 pins. Some serial ports have 25 sockets; they are usually found on older IBM PC and PC-XT machines. If you own an AT-class PC, your serial ports are probably all nine-socket

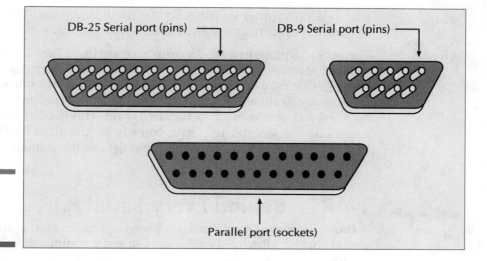

DB-25 Serial port (pins)

DB-9 Serial port (pins)

Parallel port (sockets)

Typical PC
parallel and
serial ports
Figure 1-4.

types. Your video port will be the same size and shape, but it will have nine plugs instead of nine sockets.

Standard part descriptions for port connectors refer to the gender, shape, and the number of pins or holes. A PC's parallel port is a DB-25S: "D" for the shape of the connector, "25" for the number of wires it can accept, and "S" for the sockets it shows to the world. A matching cable would have a DB-25P connector; the "P" stands for "plugs." The smaller type of serial port is a DB-9P, and requires a DB-9S cable connector.

The RS-232C Standard

If serial communication needs only one wire, why have 9-plug and 25-plug serial ports? Serial communication sends bits one at a time in just one direction. If you want to receive data at the same time you're transmitting, you need two serial wires. A third wire is needed to carry the signal ground voltage against which the voltages on the data lines are measured.

Serial ports include other wires that control the flow of data and can control a modem if one is attached. Flow control and modem control functions are the most commonly needed "extras" in a serial link, and they take up another six wires. So you need nine wires in the serial port to handle a modem and at least a nine-plug connector.

The other 16 plugs in a DB-25 connector are there "just in case." The industry standards covering serial communications describe a total of 25 wires that may be used in a standard link. The large number of wires is necessary to allow for very specialized links and computers; in reality, no serial link ever uses all 25 standard wires. This industry standard is so pervasive that serial links have come to be known as *RS-232C* links, the abbreviation for the document that defines the standard.

UARTs: Behind Every Serial Port

A *UART* (Universal Asynchronous Receiver-Transmitter) is an integrated circuit that handles most of the work in serial communication. UARTs are found in every serial port, including modem cards with serial port circuitry built into them.

All in all, a UART is an admirably busy and blessedly troublefree chip. Data arrives at the UART via an 8-bit parallel link. It must be broken down into bits, and the bits sent out through the serial port. Incoming bits must be monitored for stop/start bits and checked for parity. Inbound bits must be realigned for parallel transmission to the computer. If there's a modem connected to the serial port, the UART also monitors and controls it through separate wires specified by the RS-232C standard.

UARTs are worth a thought only if you plan to use high-speed serial links of 38,400 bps or more. Then you will want to make sure your UART is a model 16550 chip or clone, not one of the older 8520 or 16450 designs.

The two older models can store only one inbound and one outbound bit a time. If that bit isn't processed and passed on fast enough, the next bit coming in will be lost; it simply has no place to wait in the UART.

Today's 9600 and 14,400 bps modems can achieve effective throughput rates of 38,400 and 57,600 bps respectively, using data-compression techniques. But all that expensive potential is wasted if your UART can't catch bits as fast as the modem pitches them. Retransmission of corrupted data will drastically lower your throughput rate.

The 16550 UART's solution is a *data buffer,* a 16-bit "shelf" on which inbound bits can wait until the UART's circuitry gets caught up. Some companies are already making serial ports with 32-bit buffers. The way modem speeds keep inching up, these may not be a bad long-term investment.

COM Ports and IRQs

COM Ports and IRQs cause about 75 percent of all sweat, tears, and blasphemies shed during installation of communications links. Once you get COM ports and IRQs properly configured, linking actually becomes fun! So let's make this part as painless as possible.

A COM "Port" Is a Byte

A serial port must exchange data and commands with the PC it serves. It does so via the *I/O port addresses,* a section of the PC's main memory reserved for input and output. Each serial port is assigned a group of eight consecutive bits (one byte) to use for passing its output to the PC and receiving its input from the PC.

The original IBM PC was designed with port addresses for just two serial ports. One group of port addresses was given the nickname COM1 (for "COMmunications"), and the other was named COM2. As serial links grew more popular than the original PC's designers anticipated, other "unofficial" port addresses were used to support more serial ports. COM3 and COM4 are de facto standards on nearly all PCs. The various vendors have not achieved a workable consensus on what segments of main memory should be "standard" for COM5 and higher.

Avoiding Port Conflicts

Port conflicts happen when two or more serial ports try to use the same set of port addresses. You cannot assign COM1 to more than one serial port and expect things to work. It would be like assigning one telephone line to two employees; neither would be able to complete a call if both tried to dial a number at the same time.

There is an easy way to find out what port addresses are already assigned before you add another serial port.

The DOS utility program DEBUG.EXE should be in the disk directory that holds your other DOS commands (usually it's called DOS). If the DOS directory is not included in your computer's path (use the PATH command), switch to the DOS directory before typing any of the following commands.

1. Type **DEBUG** and press the [Enter] key to start DEBUG.EXE.
2. When DEBUG.EXE has loaded, you will see a hyphen to the left of your cursor instead of your usual command-line prompt.
3. Type **D40:00** and press the [Enter] key to tell DEBUG to display the contents of main memory starting at address 40:00.
4. When you are ready to quit DEBUG.EXE, type **Q** and press [Enter].

DEBUG.EXE will display several lines of numbers in response to step 3. The first line will look much like the row of numbers and letters in Figure 1-5.

The eight pairs of numbers to the left of the hyphen reveal the starting address of any active serial ports, COM1 to COM4. The preceding example shows that COM1 is being used, and is assigned to the eight bits of memory starting at address 03F8. (DEBUG displays F8 03, which is the opposite of the order in which humans usually write hexadecimal memory addresses.) COM2 is also in use and starts at 02F8, and COM3 starts at 02E8.

You can tell that COM4 is not being used because the last two pairs of numbers are 00 00, so if you needed to add a serial port to the computer used in this example, you would set its hardware to use COM4.

The pairs of numbers to the right of the hyphen show the starting port addresses for any parallel ports. Only one parallel port, LPT1, is active

DEBUG display of port address assignments
Figure 1-5.

```
0040:0000  F8 03   F8 02   E8 02   00 00-78 03   00 00 00 00 00 00
            COM1    COM2    COM3    COM4  LPT1
                                    not
```

in the preceding example. It begins at memory location 0378 (78 03 in DEBUG's terms).

Fixing Port Conflicts

You can tell if there is a port conflict by comparing what your PC *thinks* is active to what your own visual inspection tells you *should* be active. Count the serial ports on the back of your PC, whether or not anything is plugged into them. If you have an internal modem, a LAN adapter, or any other add-in cards that use serial communications, count them as well.

Your visual count should match the number of active port addresses indicated by DEBUG. If they don't match, you have a port conflict somewhere. Two (or more) of the physical ports you counted are trying to share COM1, COM2, COM3, or COM4.

Fixing port conflicts is a tedious matter of locating one of the offending ports and resetting its DIP switches or jumpers to use a vacant COM port address. A little deductive reasoning can sometimes mitigate the hassle.

The standard serial ports that came with your PC are probably set up properly. If your original equipment included one serial port, it is most likely using COM1. If two serial ports were included, assume (for now) they use COM1 and COM2.

The conflict is probably caused by an internal modem, LAN adapter, or other add-in card, even if such extras were installed by the vendor who sold you the PC. PC system vendors usually buy these cards from other vendors and add them to their PCs as needed. All too often, the vendor just sticks a card in without checking its port address settings, and you have to straighten things out.

Start with the add-in card's manual. Find the factory default settings, which should tell you what port address was set when the card was shipped. If the default setting is the same as one of your serial ports, pull the card and change it to use COM2 if you have only one serial port in use, or COM3 if you have two serial ports.

If you have two add-in cards, check the second one's settings while you have the PC open. The second card should be set so it doesn't conflict with the first add-in card or any serial ports.

If you have only two serial ports and no add-in cards, or if resetting add-in card ports doesn't work, your serial ports must be conflicting. Set one of them to COM2 and the other to COM1.

Sharing IRQs

Before attempting to converse with someone, you generally make some sound or signal to get their attention. A serial port gets the PC's attention before exchanging data. It interrupts what the PC is doing by sending a signal to a totally different memory address called an *IRQ*, for Interrupt ReQuest address.

Your PC gets such interruptions from many devices besides serial ports, so many IRQ addresses are built into each PC. They are named IRQ1, IRQ2, IRQ3, and so on, for convenient reference. IRQ3 and IRQ4 are designated for use by serial ports. If you add a third serial port, it can have COM3 all to itself, but it must share an IRQ with another serial port, unless you bend the rules and take some chances. (See "Using Three or More Ports at Once" at the end of this chapter.)

There is a simple rule for sharing IRQs: several serial devices can be assigned to one IRQ, but only one serial device can use a shared IRQ at any given time. Industry standards dictate that *COM1 and COM3 share IRQ4*, while *COM2 and COM4 share IRQ3*. So you can use two serial devices at a time, but they cannot be COM1 and COM3 or COM2 and COM4.

"Use" includes memory-resident software that is actively monitoring a serial port, even though the human operator may be doing something else. Mouse drivers are the most common culprits in IRQ conflicts. You may not be using the mouse; you may not even know the mouse driver software is in memory. But if you try to use a serial port that shares an IRQ with your mouse's serial port, it won't work as long as the mouse driver is in memory.

Since most people use a mouse only with specific programs, one solution is to write batch files that load the mouse driver just before a program is loaded, and unload the mouse driver when the program that uses it terminates. Such a batch file might look like this:

```
c:\mousware\mouse.com 2
cd c:\word\doc
```

```
word.exe
c:\mousware\mouse.com out
```

This batch file loads MOUSE.COM and tells it to use COM2 (and IRQ3). It then switches to the directory in which you store your Microsoft Word documents, and loads Word ready to use the mouse. When you exit Word, you return to the batch file, which ends by taking the mouse driver out of memory.

Using two modems, one for fax and another for data, is a good example of permissible IRQ sharing. The modems can generally use COM1 and COM3 or COM2 and COM4 without any IRQ conflicts. Most people use one modem at a time, so the IRQ is only servicing one COM port address at a time. One exception would be a memory-resident fax-receiving program, which would cause a conflict if you attempt to load a terminal program for a data session.

If your PC is linked to a LAN (Local Area Network), the driver software must remain in memory all the time. You will effectively be limited to three serial ports: one for the LAN adapter, and the two that share the IRQ that the LAN port doesn't monopolize.

Using Three or More Ports at Once

Should you ever need to use more than two serial ports at the same time, there are two handy ways to avoid IRQ conflicts:

1. "Borrow" an IRQ address normally used by another device. This borrowing is usually accomplished very easily by setting IRQs in the software that will be used with the serial port, though some serial port devices force you to set the hardware. IRQ5, for example, is designated for tape drive controllers. If you don't have a tape drive, you could use IRQ5 address 280H to service a third serial port. Other possibilities include IRQ5 3F0H (PC-XT hard disk controller) or IRQ5 278H (normally LPT2, a second printer port). Check your PC's list of interrupts and make sure you do not use an IRQ address that is supporting an existing device.

2. Buy a multiport I/O card; they cost anywhere from $150 to over $1,000. These cards provide the hardware and software necessary to let up to eight serial ports share the same IRQ address without conflict. By borrowing unused IRQ addresses as described in the

preceding paragraph, you can use more than two multiport I/O cards to get a *lot* of serial ports going at once. It is not unusual to see electronic bulletin board systems with 8, 16, 32, even 64 modems, each using its own serial port! Arnet Corp. is one of the oldest and largest makers of multiport cards; see Appendix E for Arnet's address and phone number.

A Little Knowhow Goes a Long Way

You should now understand how data is stored in the form of bits, and how electrical current can carry bits from one place to another. Remember that synchronous communication is the faster way to transmit large blocks of data in one direction, while asynchronous communication is better suited for interative, character-at-a-time data exchange.

Become familiar with the parallel and serial ports available on your PC. Identify their connectors, and make a list of what COM port and IRQ addresses the serial ports use. Check the mouse software, modems, and other serial devices connected to your PC to see if any of them are likely to conflict with others.

Most people find they need just one parallel port and at most two serial ports to meet all their linking requirements. This basic setup lets you use a printer and any two serial devices—mouse, modem, fax board, file-transfer cable, and a host of other linking add-ons—without worrying about IRQ conflicts.

Adding a third or fourth serial port is easy, as long as you think about which ports will be in constant use and which pairs of ports might be used at the same time. If you want your fax board on COM1 to be always ready to receive, forget about using COM3, unless you can assign it to an unused IRQ address. You can still use COM2 and COM4 as long as they don't try to access IRQ3 at the same time. You could install a mouse on COM2 and a modem on COM4; just don't try to use mouse-driven modem software.

Perhaps your PC is on a LAN and you keep your fax board always ready to receive. Borrowing idle IRQs or buying a multiport I/O card can still give you total linking freedom.

C H A P T E R

Hot Links

2 SHARING PRINTERS AMONG SEVERAL PCS

The sharing of printers is the most important reason to install a network, according to 80 percent of the computer managers that were surveyed by Creative Strategies International (Santa Clara, CA). A quality laser printer costs $1,500 to $4,000, so it makes sense to keep it as busy as possible.

People often buy a local area network when all they really want to do is share printers. LANs allow printer sharing, but they are really designed and intended to do much more. Buying a LAN mainly for its printer-sharing abilities is like buying a four-wheel-drive pickup truck to carry groceries. You will spend a lot more money than you have to, and much of the LAN's abilities will be wasted if all you do is share printers.

This chapter explores printer-sharing alternatives that use parallel and serial connections. Their cost ranges from about $20 to $150 per connected computer, versus $200 to over $400 per PC for a full-blown LAN. The simplest, hardware-only solutions require nothing more than plugging cables into boxes. Even the more complex, software-driven options are much easier to install and consume less of your PC's resources than any LAN.

Mechanical Printer-Sharing Switches

The simplest printer-sharing device is a *mechanical switch,* a box bearing input and output ports on its back and a knob-type switch on the front. A basic switch that lets two PCs share one printer will cost less than $75. Figure 2-1 shows front and back views of such a switch. This simple two-PC/one-printer switch is known as an A-B switch, referring to the selections you can make by turning the knob.

You will need three cables, one for each PC and one for the printer; all of them connect to the ports on the switch. A standard printer cable, with a DB-25 connector on one end and a Centronics printer connector on the other should suffice for the switch-to-printer link. Each PC-to-switch link will require a DB-25 connector on *both* ends. Be sure to get the genders right.

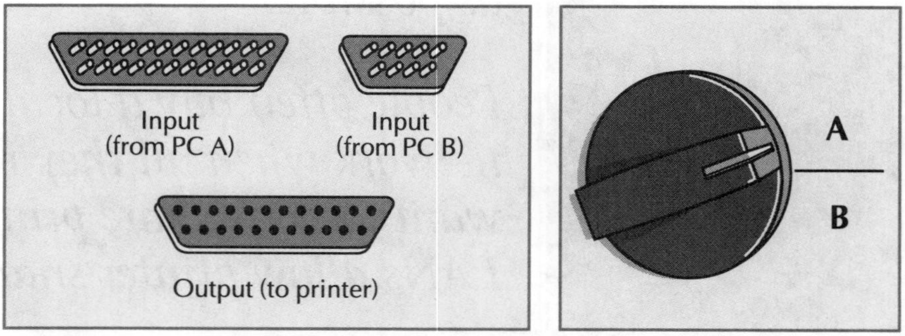

Front and back views of a mechanical switch box
Figure 2-1.

Input (from PC A)

Input (from PC B)

Output (to printer)

A

B

An A-B switch requires no changes to each PC's software or port configuration; every program that uses the printer should run fine without adjustments. But each user must remember to check the switch's setting before printing, to be sure the switch is set to link the computer to the printer. Before changing the switch setting, the user must make sure the printer is not being used by anyone else; turning the knob in the middle of someone else's print job will break that user's connection and ruin the print job.

The total amount of parallel cable between any PC and any printer should not exceed 25 feet. There is a human factor involved in this recommendation, as well as the inherent limitations of parallel communications. You really don't want to walk more than 25 feet to print a memo, do you?

You can buy mechanical switches with more ports to let several PCs share one printer, but having more than two or three users share a printer this way is impractical, especially if users are separated by room dividers or office walls. It is too difficult to run from room to room checking to be sure no one else is printing before turning that knob to your own link.

Hands-Free Printer Sharing for Just Two PCs

Xircom Corp. makes a parallel port *multiplexor* that is ideal for simple two-PC/one-printer connections. The multiplexor is a small box, about the size of a cigarette pack, that plugs into a PC's parallel port. A DB-25 connector leads to the printer, but a *second* DB-25 connector in the side of this little device lets you plug in a cable from a second PC—no knobs to turn, no stand-alone box requiring more shelf space. This Xircom device carries a list price of $95, and mail-order catalogs often sell it for $40 to $50.

Print Buffers Eliminate Waiting for a Printer

One problem with mechanical switches is that only one person can print to a given printer at a time; other users must wait their turns and keep checking to see when the printer is free. A lot of productive work time can be lost.

Buffered printer-sharing devices—*print buffers* for short—can take a print job off your PC's hands, store it until the desired printer is available, and print your document while you are doing something else. The data intended for the printer is stored in a bank of random access memory (RAM) built into the print buffer. Buffers can be purchased with anywhere from 32K (kilobytes) to 8MB (megabytes) of memory. How much buffer RAM you need depends on the average size of the documents you print and how many users will share a printer.

Think of a print buffer as a secretary you share with several other people. When you want to submit a draft document for typing, you don't stand around waiting for the secretary to finish typing another document; you just put your draft in an In basket and get back to work. The secretary normally takes jobs from the basket in the order they are received, though some jobs may be tagged as high priorities and get bumped to the head of the line.

Buffering makes printer sharing totally transparent to the user, once a printer is selected and configured for that user's job. You print from any application software or the DOS command line exactly as you would if you had your very own printer. Several PCs can send print jobs to a buffer at the same time, so there is no waiting for an available printer. Figure 2-2 shows three PCs sharing two printers via a print buffer.

Print buffers usually come with software that lets a user select a printer, choose fonts, view the number and size of print jobs ahead of the user's print job, and control other aspects of the print buffer's operation. Control software is often *memory resident,* meaning that it is kept in memory even when another program is loaded. A memory-resident program can be accessed at any time by pressing a particular combination of keys, called *hot keys*. This allows a user to load a word processor, spreadsheet, or other application software, and call up the print buffer's program to select printers, load fonts, and so on, without exiting the main program.

Print buffers cost a bit more than switches. Expect to pay $100 to $150 per computer or printer that will be linked. Print buffers can be purchased with anywhere from 4 to 12 ports for computers and printers.

Owners of Hewlett-Packard LaserJet printers might be interested in a line of print-buffering devices from Extended Systems, Inc. (Boise, ID),

2

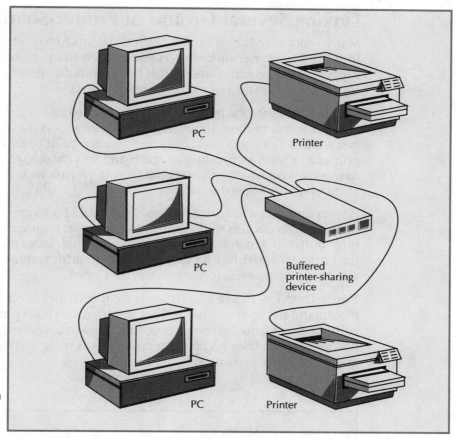

The print buffer
stores the print
jobs and
distributes them
Figure 2-2.

that plug into the optional input/output ports found on HP LaserJet
Series II and III printers. These Sharespool print buffers are
exceptionally easy to install and use. They take up no room at all
compared to desktop print buffers, and use inexpensive telephone-style
cables and modular plugs instead of bulky DB-style cables and
connectors. Sharespool devices can let up to eight PCs share one
LaserJet, at a cost of $495 to $895 per Sharespool device.

Linking Several Groups of Printer-Sharing Users

Many vendors sell print buffers that can be linked to each other, forming a larger network of users and printers than one buffer can support. Vendors often refer to this buffer-to-buffer linking as *cascading*. Figure 2-3 illustrates a cascaded group of buffers.

The link between one buffer and another in Figure 2-3 gives users in group A access to the printers in group B, and vice versa. This single cascade link is a bottleneck; only one user can print to another group's printer at a time. Depending on the brand you choose, you may be able to speed up transbuffer throughput by using a parallel link or a vendor's proprietary high-speed serial link.

If you plan to cascade print buffers, you should try to configure them so that users have access to the printer(s) they most frequently use on the print buffer to which they are directly connected. Large files will tie up the buffer-to-buffer link longer, so users who print graphics files should also have direct access to the printers they need.

Notice User A in Figure 2-3. This user frequently needs access to the plotter and the laser printer, so User A is linked to both print buffers without going through the cascade link. This arrangement ties up two printer ports on User A's computer, but avoids tying up the transbuffer link when other users need it.

A cascaded group of buffers; User A has direct access to both buffers
Figure 2-3.

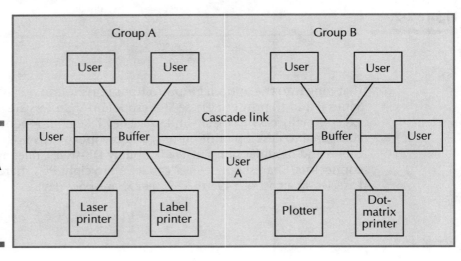

Shared Printers Can Be Overworked

When a printer is shared among several users, it may need to be faster and more durable than a single-user printer. A typical one-user laser printer might print four to eight pages per minute and require a replacement print drum every 10,000 pages or so. Printers are also rated according to how many pages per month they should handle; overworking a printer will lead to more frequent breakdowns and service calls. Printers intended for sharing may need to be as fast as 17 to 25 pages per minute, go 25,000 to 35,000 pages between drum changes, and be rated for 20,000 to 30,000 pages per month.

2

Cables and Connectors for Printer Sharing

While all of the printer-sharing options discussed in this chapter use either parallel or serial communications links, the choice of hardware to make the physical connections is not that simple. The trend toward linking more and more different computers and devices has given rise to a bewildering array of cabling schemes. A standard RS-232C cable with DB-type connectors on each end, like the one you probably use to link one printer to one PC, is only one of many possibilities.

Most printer-sharing products use a standard parallel link from the device to a printer. The DB-25 connectors on most printers are female. The corresponding connector on the printer-sharing device should be of the opposite gender, so you can use standard printer cables that come with opposite gender connectors on each end. If the device and printer connectors are the same gender, you can purchase a gender-changing adapter for the printer or the device; these cost about $7 each. Female-to-male gender changers have male connectors on both ends; male-to-female adapters have female connectors on both ends.

The links from PCs to switching devices can include any combination of parallel and serial ports you need. The distance from PC to printer-sharing device is the primary consideration when choosing serial or parallel links. Generally, you should use parallel links for relatively short PC-to-device connections to maximize data transmission speed. Use serial links for longer connections to maximize reliability and minimize cable costs.

Vendors make widely varying claims for the range and speed of their parallel and serial links. Most recommend parallel links of less than 30 feet, while a few dare you to try 100 or even 400 feet of parallel cable. Longer cables invariably require substantially slower data transmission speeds. You may get reliable 100-foot connections at 19,200 bps, but don't expect 115,200 bps over that much parallel cable unless you invest in optional booster units that replenish and clean up signals along the way. Ask vendors if they sell such boosters for long links

The type of cable used for serial links in printer-sharing devices can vary a great deal. The important thing is to buy exactly the type of cable your printer-sharing device requires. Owner's manuals usually provide detailed specifications, including wiring diagrams.

Some devices, like the Sharespool, use very inexpensive telephone-style cable with modular plugs. This cabling scheme can save money versus RS-232C cable. Devices that use telephone-style cable will have modular jacks instead of DB-9 or DB-25 connectors, so you can just plug either end of the cable directly into the device. You will need a DB-to-modular adapter for each PC's serial port to accommodate the plug-in cable; these cost about $10 each, reducing or reversing the cost advantage of telephone-style wire over short distances.

Mix of Print Jobs Affects Productivity

Printers can be configured for sharing in any way that's convenient; the question is, "Convenient for whom?" When deciding where printers will be located in relation to the users they serve and who will have access to which printer(s), you should consider the human as well as the electronic aspects of printer sharing. The mixture of print jobs sent to a given printer, its distance from the person(s) who need the printed output, and a printer's impact on its immediate environment are every bit as important as the hardware and software you choose.

If users will be responsible for retrieving their own printouts, no one should be more than a few dozen paces from the printer. The printer should be located where users can get to it without parading through other people's work area.

If one person will be assigned the job of retrieving printouts and distributing them to their owners, that person needs to be near the printer. If the printer is a noisy dot-matrix type, a printer enclosure may be necessary to muffle the sound. The selected employee should be someone whose constant presence at a desk is not required; don't give this job to your receptionist!

Changing paper trays can be a nuisance in a shared-printer environment. You can try to identify groups of users who all print on the same type of paper and assign them to one printer. Scheduling batches of jobs that all require the same type of paper or envelope can also help maintain productivity. Many printers can be purchased with multiple paper trays, and the print-buffer software can be used to select the appropriate tray for a specific job.

Checklist for Buying a Printer-Sharing Device

Here are some important questions to consider when deciding on a printer-sharing device:

+ How many PCs and how many printers will be linked?

+ Will parallel links work throughout the network, or will you need serial links for the longest stretches?

+ If you want a buffer, how much RAM should it have?

+ What kind(s) of cables and connectors can you use?

+ Is your printer fast and durable enough to support the number of users and the kinds of print jobs contemplated?

+ If you need to cascade buffers, which users will belong to which buffer groups?

+ Where should each printer be located? Who will retrieve printouts, change paper trays, and load new paper?

Summary: Printer Sharing Is a Good Start on Linking

If you are unaccustomed to "thinking linking," printer sharing is an excellent way to ease into it. The benefits are immediate and substantial; it's hard to lose money by buying a printer-sharing solution instead of a printer for every desk. The technical and installation considerations are relatively simple, but offer plenty of practice in network planning and vendor selection. You might even find that your linking needs are totally satisfied by print buffers.

C H A P T E R

Hot Links

3

LINKING PCS TO EXCHANGE FILES AND ELECTRONIC MAIL

Exchanging files between PCs is the second most common reason for wanting to link computers. (Peripheral sharing is the leader by a wide margin.) File exchange is analogous to photocopying as a method of distributing data. File exchange differs from file sharing (discussed in Chapter 4). In file sharing, you access files on a network. In file exchange, you actually copy a file to the receiver's computer system on or off of a network.

The following examples illustrate some common file-exchange applications.

Before leaving on a road trip, you probably photocopy reports, price lists, and other essential documents and then toss them in your briefcase. File-exchange links let you copy essential files to a laptop computer, even if your desktop PC's floppy disk won't fit your laptop's drive.

Sending a copy of a document to a colleague lets both of you view the document while you discuss it. Each of you can edit the document at the same time, and the changes can be merged into one final document later. File exchange is easier and faster than the traditional photocopying, mailing, and retyping process. Modems let you perform file exchanges over telephone lines, so it doesn't matter if your colleague is in your office or thousands of miles away.

File-exchange software can "clone" exact copies of disks in one operation. New employees generally need a set of standard documents that everyone in their department uses: policy and procedure manuals, price lists, form letters, telephone directories, and so on. A computer-driven work group also needs standard application software on every workstation, and it is very helpful if every PC's hard disk directories and configuration files are set up in the same way.

File exchange lets you synchronize files on different PCs so that each contains the most recent version of files common to all machines. You can ensure that every workstation always contains the latest versions of reports, price lists, form letters, and other constantly changing documents.

File exchange can also solve compatibility problems in a firm that has several types of computers. Exchanging files between a desktop computer with 5 1/4-inch floppy drives and a laptop with a 3 1/2-inch drive is impossible using floppy disks, but easy with just a cable and some software. Macintosh, MS-DOS, UNIX, and mainframe machines can swap data over wires, even though one disk drive cannot read what another writes.

Electronic mail is a particularly versatile and cost-effective type of file exchange. E-mail can now include graphics images, as well as text. Even oral comments can be digitized and attached to electronic documents, to be played back by the receiver(s). Packaging, postage, and courier expenses, even the cost of paper, ink, and intraoffice delivery labor, can be saved using e-mail. Many organizations gain competitive advantages as well as saving money. Near-instantaneous delivery of information makes a company more adaptable, more unified, and more responsive to its customers' ever-changing needs.

These functions, and peripheral-sharing tasks described in Chapter 2, can be performed over ordinary parallel and serial links. The cost can be under $100 per PC or peripheral, half the cost of the lowest priced LAN. Only one central switch is needed to connect all the computers and peripherals, instead of a LAN adapter for each workstation. You don't need a dedicated server computer to tie all the components together. You can hook a printer, modem, or other peripheral directly into the network; it needn't be attached to a computer served by a LAN.

Simultaneous file sharing is about the only feature LANs offer that file-exchange and peripheral-sharing networks lack. If you don't need to have several users access the same data file at the same time, you can save a great deal of money and time with the solutions in this chapter.

Setting Up the Physical Links

File-exchange links can be quite simple, as in the case of temporarily connecting a laptop computer to a desktop machine with a short cable. You can also set up a network of serial cables that allows every PC in your office to link with any other as needed. Like printer-sharing devices, file-exchange hardware comes in many forms.

A One-to-One Connection

Two computers can be connected by a serial cable. Let's call the computer at which you will be sitting and directing file exchanges the *local* computer, and the other one the *remote* computer.

It is not necessary to use the same serial port addresses on both computers. The local computer can be using COM1, while the remote PC is using COM2. But you *will* need to know both port addresses when it's time to install software; write them down as you connect the cables.

A parallel link, because it moves several bits at once, would transfer data about two to four times faster than a serial link. You can generally use a parallel connection if the distance a file must travel is less than 25 feet.

Standard straight-through parallel cables with DB-25 connectors can be used.

Many PCs come equipped with only one parallel port, and most people already have a printer plugged into it. If you exchange files often, it can become tedious to unplug the printer cable, plug in the file-transfer cable, and restore the printer connection again. Xircom Corp. makes a *parallel port switcher,* a clever little adapter that lets you leave both printer cable and file-transfer cable plugged into one parallel port at all times. The switcher is about the size of a cigarette pack, and costs about $40; see Appendix E for Xircom's address.

Data Switches for Low-Cost Networking of Up to 12 PCs and Peripherals

Very small groups of two to four computers might get by with direct connections between all PCs, but if you run a cable from your PC to two or three others, you will quickly run out of parallel and serial ports. Such a system also creates an unsightly and hazardous tangle of wires running from each desk across the work area.

A *data switch* lets you link any two ports connected to it on demand. It works much like the telephone line switch in your office or at the telephone company's central office. Only one wire runs from each PC to the data switch, just as the phone on your desk uses just one wire. If you need a connection to the accounting department's computer, you just "dial" that department, and the data switch takes care of making the physical link. You can use this link just like a direct port-to-port connection.

Data switches can also link printers, modems, and other peripherals to computers. Many data switches include buffer memory, so they can perform the duties of print buffers. Yet they cost about the same as dedicated print buffers, generally $100 to $200 per PC, and substantially less than the $200 to $400 initial investment needed for a high-speed local area network.

Data Switch Speeds and Range

All data switches use parallel and serial communications methods, so compared to LANs they are slower and limited in range. But over distances of up to 1500 feet, many organizations find they can accomplish everything they need to do with data switches.

The range of data switch links generally is measured from a PC to the switch and from the switch to another PC or peripheral device. A data switch that boosts a signal before sending it to its destination will extend the total range from one end of a link to another. Some data switches, like the Buffalo Products' SL-512, claim to achieve parallel links of up to 400 feet and serial links up to 1500 feet. Most data switches are rated reliable up to 15 to 30 feet for parallel links, and up to about 100 feet for serial links.

Transmission speed through a data switch will vary a great deal, depending on how many PCs are using the switch at a given moment, the tasks they are performing, the length of each link, and whether the link is a parallel or serial connection. A data switch simultaneously accepting printer input from four to six PCs over serial links may need to run at 19,200 bps or slower to ensure reliable transmission. A 30-foot parallel link may transfer data files from one PC to another at up to 750,000 bps, if it is the only connection in use.

Cables Can Be a Major Variable Cost

LAN cables generally cost at least $0.40 per foot. Data switches can use cabling schemes that cost as little as $0.10 per foot or as much as $0.25 per foot. The wiring scheme a data switch supports can have a great impact on the final cost of your network. Standard parallel cables are generally used for switch-to-printer connections, but PC-to-switch links may use one of three types of cable: straight through, null modem, or telephone style.

Computer-style parallel or serial cables are generally the most costly; they may have to be wired straight through or crossed over as null modem cables. Serial links can also use inexpensive four-wire telephone cable, or slightly more expensive six-wire or eight-wire telephone cable. A 100-foot cable can cost anywhere from $17.00 to $174, depending on the wiring scheme it uses.

The connectors required on each end of the cable also influence cost. Telephone-wire links require a DB-25 or DB-9 connector on the PC side and a modular phone type of jack on the cable side. Such nonstandard adapters cost about $10 each at most electronic stores.

Software for File Exchange: Introducing LapLink Pro

All data switches come with software specifically designed for selecting the connection you want. The more sophisticated data switches include basic file exchange, e-mail, and printer-control software, but these utilities are seldom the most powerful or convenient of their types. Third-party file-exchange software is usually required for the more sophisticated file-exchange applications, like disk cloning, synchronizing files, or automating incremental backups.

The available software ranges from very simple command-line utilities, similar to the DOS COPY command, to powerful programs like LapLink Pro. This chapter will use LapLink to illustrate the uses of file-exchange links because it is full featured and it is able to load itself on a remote machine (something that others are bound to pick up on). Other brands of file-transfer software and their vendors can be found in Appendix E, "Resource Directory."

Getting Help with Port Settings

File-transfer programs try to spare you the agony of identifying and setting up your computer's various parallel and serial ports. When you install LapLink, it automatically scans your computer to determine what ports are available, and tests the hardware links to determine the highest speeds at which they can operate. LapLink's Port/Modem Setup screen summarizes information about the ports that LapLink detects.

Parallel and serial ports are shown, along with each port's status. "Enabled" means LapLink has found a physical port that is using port addresses COM1, LPT1, and so on. LapLink assumes such active ports are available for it to use, but there may be some ports you do not want LapLink to use. If you have a printer attached to LPT1, for example, you don't want LapLink trying to exchange files with your printer. You can tell LapLink to ignore any port without physically disabling the port.

LapLink automatically tries to communicate at the highest speed a serial link can support. Noisy conditions on the cable connecting the two computers may force you to select a lower speed. LapLink lets you choose one of nine speeds, ranging from 300 to 115,200 bps.

Polling Avoids IRQ Conflicts

The official IBM PC standards support only COM1 and COM2, with IRQ4 supporting COM1, and IRQ3 supporting COM2. If you have added a third serial port using COM3, it ordinarily must share IRQ4 with COM1; COM4 would share IRQ3 with COM2. The possibility of IRQ conflicts can be avoided in one of three ways:

1. Disable one of the potentially conflicting ports while you are using the other.

2. "Borrow" an unused IRQ. LapLink thoughtfully provides this option by allowing you to designate IRQ5 or IRQ7 to serve a serial port. Be sure no other hardware or software is using the chosen IRQ.

3. Use serial port "polling" to avoid IRQs altogether.

The first two options are discussed in Chapter 1. Polling is not a standard feature of MS-DOS computers. It is programmed into LapLink, so let's discuss it here.

Ordinarily, it is the responsibility of the serial port to let the CPU know when the port needs attention; that is the function of the Interrupt ReQuest or IRQ. Software like LapLink assumes responsibility for checking each serial port at regular intervals to see if it needs attention. LapLink *polls* each port in turn, effectively asking the port, "Do you have any data for the CPU, or are you free to take data from the CPU?" There is no need for the port to interrupt the CPU, therefore IRQs are not used and IRQ conflicts cannot arise.

Installing LapLink on a Remote Computer

File-exchange software must be installed on the local *and* the remote computers. File exchange is like a game of catch; it takes at least two players, alternately pitching and catching. Often you can just sit down at the remote computer, install the exchange software, and then return to your local machine.

But the remote computer may not have a disk drive that can accept your disk, or the remote PC may be inconveniently far away. LapLink's ability to install itself through a serial link comes in very handy under such circumstances.

The first step is to tell LapLink which serial ports to use. The "From Local Port" list is used to specify the cable on your local computer. "To Remote Port" tells LapLink where the serial cable ends on the remote computer.

After defining and naming the link, select the Install command. A box will be displayed showing how to set up the remote PC to receive LapLink. Remember, the remote computer does not have LapLink installed yet. But something must "catch" what you are about to "pitch" over the serial cable. The "catcher" will be MS-DOS.

The following steps are performed on the remote computer to prepare it to receive LapLink. Usually someone at the remote computer will perform these functions while you remain at the local computer's console.

1. Create a subdirectory to receive LapLink and log into that directory.
2. Enter the following commands at the DOS prompt:

```
MODE COMx:2400,N,8,1

CTTY COMx
```

   where *x* represents the number of the COM port address being used, for example, COM1 or COM2. Substitute the appropriate port address in these commands.

The MODE command sets the baud rate and communications settings of the serial port: 2400 bps, no parity, eight data bits, one stop bit.

The CTTY command redirects the remote computer's input and output to the serial port, instead of the keyboard and monitor. After entering the CTTY command, you will find the computer will no longer respond to any more keyboard commands; its attention is now on the serial port.

After the remote PC is set up to receive, select OK on the *local* computer's Install screen to proceed with the remote installation. LapLink transmits itself over the serial link to the remote computer's current drive and directory.

When the remote installation is complete, you will have LapLink up and running on both PCs. Now you are ready to exchange some files between them.

Copying and Moving Files

The essence of file exchange is making a copy of a *source* file and placing the copy at a new *target* location. If the original file is then deleted, the file has effectively been *moved,* not just copied. Anyone who has used MS-DOS a few times knows how the COPY and DEL commands work.

Managing large-scale file exchanges is rather tedious and error prone using just the COPY and DEL commands. Good file-exchange software provides shortcuts and safeguards that make file exchange much easier. The following sections describe some of the features to look for in your file-exchange software.

Directory Viewing and Navigation

One of the most important features is the ability to see simultaneously the files you plan to copy and the place they will end up. LapLink and other programs have this feature.

A tree diagram shows all subdirectories on a disk, making it easy to find and move to the subdirectory you want. All the files in a directory, including its subdirectories and *their* files, can be selected by highlighting a directory and pressing a key.

Restricting Selections to Specific Files

Most often you will want to copy only certain files in a directory or branch of a directory tree, while leaving other files uncopied. For example, you may want to make backup copies of only the document files in your word processor's subdirectory, while excluding the executable files, spell-checker data files, and printer configuration files. You should be able to do this by matching filename patterns or dates.

A *file mask* uses DOS wildcard characters to filter out everything that does not match a filename pattern. Some examples of file masks include

✦ *.TXT, which selects files whose extension is TXT, for example, LETTER.TXT.

✦ BUDGET??.DOC, which selects files whose first six characters are "BUDGET" and whose extension is DOC. The two characters represented by question marks may or may not exist; this mask would select BUDGET.DOC, BUDGET1.DOC, or BUDGET12.DOC.

Date masks let you select files created or altered on or after a given date or between two dates, and exclude all others from the copy process. Selection by date(s) saves time when making backup copies, since you need only copy files that have changed or been created since the last backup.

Sometimes it is easier to specify which files should *not* be copied than to describe all the file patterns that *should* be copied. The ability to reverse a selection lets you choose files by whichever method is easier, then effectively say, "I want to copy everything *except* these files."

Checking the Size of Selected Files and Available Space

Running out of space on the target disk in the middle of a copy operation can be very frustrating. You should be able to check the total size of the group of files you have selected before executing a copy command, and also see how many bytes of storage space are available on the target drive.

Setting Copy Options

Your software should let you specify how a copy or move operation will take place. The most critical options are these:

1. Should files in subdirectories under the current one be included in the copy/move selection?
2. Should newer source files overwrite older target files of the same name?
3. Should the software pause and ask you for confirmation before overwriting existing files?
4. Should read-only files in the target drive be overwritten if necessary?
5. Should all selected files be copied, or only files whose names already exist in the target?

When subdirectories are included, selecting one directory to be copied automatically selects all its subdirectories too. When the copy is executed, subdirectories will be created on the target disk if they do not already exist. If a filename pattern or date range filter is in effect, it affects files in the subdirectories as well as the selected directory.

Option 2 asks which version of a file that exists in both the source and target drives should end up in the target drive, the older one or the newer one? The decision will be based on the date and time stamp added by each computer when a file is created or altered; it's important that both computers' clocks be accurate in order for this option to be effective.

Option 4 deals with files whose read-only attributes have been switched on. Ordinarily, you cannot copy over a read-only file, but some file-transfer software will ignore the read-only attribute if you tell it to do so. The first time you make a backup copy of your hard disk, you probably will want to copy read-only files as well as all others. Thereafter, you may want to recopy a read-only file onto your backup disk(s) if the information it contains has changed.

Option 5 can save a great deal of time when making backup copies. It effectively tells your file-exchange software, "I only want to update files that I have copied to this target before." Any files that do not already exist on the target drive will be ignored.

Cloning Entire Drives

Cloning re-creates a disk drive's entire structure on another drive. Directory trees and the files they contain are reproduced exactly on the target drive. Cloning is especially useful in setting up new computers in a homogeneous work group such as a sales or data-entry department. PC administrators find it much easier to manage and troubleshoot groups of identically configured computers.

Cloning destroys all data and directory structures previously resident on the target disk. Cloning also copies all hidden, read-only, and system files from the source to the target disk, so if you plan to clone a bootable drive (one that contains the hidden system files of the MS-DOS operating system), the target disk must be formatted using the same version of MS-DOS as the source drive.

Synchronizing Files on Different PCs

Let's suppose you copied some documents from your desktop PC to your laptop several weeks ago. While on the road with the laptop, you changed a few numbers in a spreadsheet, created a few new documents, and perhaps updated some entries in your address book. Back at the office, you continued creating and changing files on your desktop machine.

Now you want to make sure that both machines have the latest versions of the files they have in common, and that any files missing from one machine are copied from the other. In other words, you want to get both computers back in synch with each other.

File synchronizing is a two-way update performed in one operation. The files on one machine are compared to those on the other, and a list is made of files that already exist on both computers. Then the newer version of a file is copied from one machine to the other. Any files that exist on one machine but not on the other will be copied to the second computer. After a file synchronization, both machines will have the same files and the latest versions of files that previously existed on both machines.

Modems Make Long-Distance File Exchanges Possible

Most high-end file-exchange programs can use modems to link computers over normal telephone lines. Then it no longer matters whether the linked PCs are in the same room or literally an ocean apart; you can copy and move files, clone or synchronize disks, and even install your file-exchange software on a remote computer no matter how far away it may be.

Since modem links are always serial connections, and voice-grade telephone lines are relatively noisy, you will be limited to speeds of 9600 bps at best. It takes over 20 minutes to transmit a 1.2MB high-density floppy disk at 9600 bps, so you probably won't do large file exchanges over long distances very often. But modems can save the day when you need to link up with a computer that's miles away.

Modems have many more uses, which will be covered in Chapter 5.

Electronic Mail: Person-to-Person File Exchange

Transfer software focuses on managing computer-to-computer file exchanges; the emphasis is on subdirectories and filenames. But electronic mail—a specialized form of file exchange—is centered on the people who use computers.

E-mail uses the same hardware links previously discussed. You can send e-mail using file-exchange software like LapLink. Just write a letter using any word processor, load LapLink, and copy your letter to the addressee's computer. If the letter references a spreadsheet file, you would probably copy that at the same time.

3

What's missing from this picture is the personal touch. LapLink copied files to a computer; it did not deliver a message to a person. Your letter and attached spreadsheet might sit on Joe's hard drive forever. E-mail software should include at least these personal touches:

✦ An address book listing the people with whom you correspond

✦ An In basket for mail you receive and an Out basket for mail you intend to send

✦ Writing and reading facilities for composing mail and viewing mail you receive

When you write an e-mail message, the address book lets you look up the name and network "address" of the intended receiver. When e-mail is sent, the software automatically chooses the right hardware link and transfers your text file message to the addressee's computer. In and Out "baskets" are typically subdirectories set up specifically for incoming and outgoing mail. Most e-mail programs include very simple text editing utilities, but also let you substitute your favorite word processor for their generic editors. Mail in your In basket can be listed by sender's name, date, subject, and often by priority. You can then skim your waiting mail and view letters onscreen in any order.

Elementary e-mail systems like the one described in the preceding paragraph are often bundled with data switches. More sophisticated e-mail software may include features like these:

✦ *Group distribution lists* Adding a one- or two-letter code to an address book record makes it part of a group of records. Now one e-mail message can be written, and automatically distributed to every person in a group.

✦ *File attachments*   Just as you might staple a cover letter to a thick document, an e-mail message can be attached to a spreadsheet, graphics file, a binary program file, or even a digitized sound file, addressed to one or more recipients. Wherever the e-mail is delivered, the attached file(s) accompany it. As many as 64 files can be attached to a single message in some e-mail systems.

✦ *Message threading*   The subject field of an e-mail message forms a logical link between the original message and replies written to it. Such "threads" of messages form the fabric of *bulletin board systems,* discussion groups in which everyone's input is electronically preserved. Any new participant can start at the original message or at any point in the thread of replies, moving forward or backward to review what has been said before.

Large e-mail systems may include hundreds or thousands of users. Such systems usually run on a LAN, using products like cc:Mail, Microsoft Windows for Workgroups, Netware Lite, and Moses Promised LAN, and all messages are stored in a central database rather than distributed all over the network. Users can copy certain messages to their own In baskets.

Summary: File Exchange and Peripheral Sharing May Be All You Need

A lot can be done with parallel and serial links, fairly simple devices like print buffers and data switches, and the right software. File-exchange and peripheral-sharing links are easy to install and inexpensive compared to full-blown media-sharing LANs. The speeds and range of such links are adequate for 95 percent of small business networking needs. Even large organizations find that most of their work is done in fairly small work groups of fewer than 20 users, where print buffers and data switches provide all the linking power necessary.

Hot Links

C H A P T E R

Hot Links

4

SHARING FILES: THREE TYPES OF LOCAL AREA NETWORKS

The next step beyond file-exchange linking is a dramatic one. For years, the PC market had fostered a very personal approach to computing, whereby a user has all the software needed on the hard disk; access to remote databases and files was not a standard mode of operation. That methodology is quickly changing as more and more PCs are being networked and files are shared between users on the net.

51

File sharing makes one copy of a file accessible to remote users. Compare that to file exchange, in which a remote file must be copied to your local PC before you can do anything with it. Here are just a few examples of things file sharing can do that file exchange cannot:

✦ Read or edit a document without taking time to copy it

✦ Run an application program such as Lotus 1-2-3 on your local machine, even though the program is on someone else's hard drive

✦ Let several users add, change, or delete records in a single database file at the same time

Working on a file without copying it saves a lot of time. Even at a serial port's top speed of 115,000 bps, a 1MB spreadsheet or database file would take roughly two minutes to copy from one machine to another. Then you might have to copy it back to the original machine when you finished; four minutes is a long time just to open and save a file!

File sharing conserves disk space. Large database files do not have to be duplicated on every PC that needs access to them. One user whose hard drive fills up can make use of surplus capacity on any other user's drive.

Tracking different versions of a file becomes unnecessary. Changing everyone's price list, for instance, becomes a simple matter of replacing one file on one disk. Everyone who shares access to that file instantly begins using the new version.

Maintaining security is simplified; there is only one copy of sensitive data to be guarded. Some organizations eliminate floppy disk drives from most PCs so confidential data cannot be copied and slipped out the door. Such *diskless workstations* are also cheaper and more compact than normal PCs. You could have a different problem with security however. You might not be able to (or might forget to) lock files or records that can be tampered with.

The ability to run remote software is especially valuable, because one copy of an application program can be shared by several users. Multiuser versions of programs allow several people to simultaneously run one copy of a spreadsheet, database manager, word processor, and so on. Generally, the cost per user of a multiuser package will be less than the cost of buying everyone a single-user copy, particularly if some users only occasionally need the program.

4

Even software designed and licensed for only one user at a time often can be shared by several people, if they are able to wait their turns. (Check the vendor's license agreement to see if it permits such use. If not, you may want to shop for a more liberal alternative to that package.)

Simultaneous multiuser access to data files is often essential in database work environments. Sales reps can check the availability of products at the same time inventory clerks are updating shipment and stock records. Customer service reps can access any client's record, so it becomes unimportant which rep answers a client's call. Airline reservation systems, with constantly changing prices, schedules, and seat assignments, would be impossible to manage if reservationists could not all access one database file.

All of these capabilities and others are found in *Local Area Networks*. LANs provide file-sharing, file-exchange, peripheral-sharing, and electronic-mail capabilities for computers that may be up to one mile apart.

NOTE: A LAN may link just two PCs across a room, or it may include over a thousand computers and assorted peripherals in several buildings.

Large LANs (20 or more linked computers, or *nodes*) are necessarily expensive and complicated to install and maintain. Data must move across a LAN much faster than ordinary serial and parallel links can handle, if only because many more people are trying to use the network at the same time. The hardware that carries LAN traffic costs ten or more times the serial or parallel ports and cables it replaces. The software that manages LAN traffic is far more complicated than printer-sharing or file-exchange software. Generally, at least one full-time employee must be trained and dedicated to running the administrative side of a LAN. Users also require extra training to take advantage of a LAN's capabilities.

Many products promising LAN performance without the cost and complications described in the preceding paragraph have hit the market in recent years. Small businesses that lack the budgets and staff to support a traditional LAN's appetites find these "easy LANs" tempting, but prospective buyers need to know the limitations of these products. Very few deliver all of the file-sharing capabilities of a full-blown LAN.

This chapter describes three distinct types of file sharing, which require progressively more expensive and complicated solutions. It describes some low-cost alternatives to full-featured LANs, including two that are represented on the disk that comes with this book. The three major types of LAN hardware systems—Ethernet, ARCnet, and Token-Ring—are compared on the basis of cost, performance, and ease of installation. The pros and cons of peer-to-peer LANs versus client/server LANs round out this tour de force.

There Are Different Degrees of "Shareability"

Most people assume file sharing means several users can edit the same file at the same time. But "access to remote files" can mean any or all of three things:

1. *Read/write access* Data files can be opened and viewed (read) by remote users. Optionally, remote users may be able to edit, create, or delete files (write privileges).

2. *Remote execution* It is one thing to open a remote document using the copy of WordPerfect on your local PC, and quite a different matter to start a copy of WordPerfect that resides on someone else's hard drive.

3. *Multiuser access* Two or more users can read, write, or execute the same copy of a file at the same time. This is the definition most people use when they think of file sharing.

Each level of file sharing creates more traffic over a network than the one before it. For example, remote read-only access is predominantly one-way; only file-open, file-close, and document-navigation commands need be transmitted from the local PC to the remote. However, when you edit a remote document, the altered data created in your local PC's memory also must make the trip and be fitted into the remote document. Remote execution and multiuser access demand even more data movement over a network.

The more users there are on a LAN performing higher-level file-sharing tasks, the slower everyone's work proceeds. The solution is to increase the data-transfer speed. LAN ports and cables should support speeds of at least two million bits per second if multiuser access to program or data files is required.

The software that drives a file-sharing network also becomes more complicated and costly, depending on the level of access required. Desk Connect, one of the programs included with this book, provides basic read/write access to a remote hard drive via a serial cable. Novell NetWare 3.*X*, the leading full-featured local area network, will cost you about $300 to $600 per PC, including software, network adapter card, and EtherNet cable. NetWare moves data at ten million bps or faster, and can support hundreds of simultaneous users performing the full range of LAN tasks.

4

Zero-Slot LANs: Don't Believe It Till You See It

In between basic disk-sharing products such as Desk Connect and high-speed LANs that provide everything from printer sharing to simultaneous multiuser access, lies a group of products commonly called *zero-slot LANs*, or ZSLs for short. ZSLs use serial or parallel ports and cables, so they do not require an expansion slot for an adapter card; hence the "zero-slot" part of their name.

Most ZSLs do not qualify as true LANs, because they do not permit file sharing of any kind. However, they are very convenient peripheral-sharing and file-exchange solutions. Some ZSLs, like LANtastic /Z from Artisoft, Inc., also include impressive electronic-mail facilities.

Virtual Devices: Making Remote Resources Local

A ZSL lets you treat the resources of remote computers exactly as if they were your own. It's as if your computer suddenly acquired more disk drives, a second printer, a new modem, and so on. ZSLs do this by assigning the names of unused devices on your local PC to devices on remote computers. You may then issue commands to these *virtual devices* by referencing the local names you have assigned to them.

NOTE: Virtual means "being so in effect, though not in actual fact or name."

For example, if you have one printer attached to your local machine, it is probably using the parallel port address LPT1. If you connected a second printer to your computer, it would most likely use LPT2. Assume your PC is linked to a remote computer via a ZSL. You can assign the name LPT2 to the printer attached to the remote computer. Now, whenever you print to LPT2, the ZSL software intercepts the print job and passes it over the cable to the printer attached to the remote computer, *not* to the parallel port your PC "thinks" is using LPT2. LPT2 is "not in actual fact" your second printer, but it behaves as if it were.

The remote computer's drive C could be your drive D, giving you complete access to the remote computer's hard drive. A subdirectory on the remote computer could be assigned a single virtual drive letter on your machine, for example, C:\PROGRAMS\WORDPERFECT\DOCS might become just drive D to you. Assigning drive letters to subdirectories restricts access to a remote drive; it also lets you access the remote subdirectory by entering just a single letter instead of the entire path name.

Having virtual drives makes it very easy to copy, delete, or move files between PCs, using familiar DOS commands. But it can take 15 seconds to transfer a 50K file over a serial link; large file transfers might call for a coffee break. Fortunately, most modern ZSL software performs file transfers and print jobs in the background, so you can do other work while the data creeps across the cable.

High-Speed LANs

Practical file sharing for groups of three or more computers demands higher data-transfer speeds than parallel or serial links can provide. Physical links with rated maximum speeds of over two million bits per second are generally considered adequate for file sharing, remote execution, and multiuser access. Such speed requires a whole new way of doing things, adding another layer of complexity and cost to the network.

Every LAN includes three components that affect its cost and performance:

4

+ Adapter cards, which directly communicate with the computers, send data out over the LAN, and receive incoming data from other computers and peripherals on the LAN

+ Cables that connect the ports and carry data between computers

+ LAN operating system software, which manages the data traffic on the LAN, controls who has access to files and peripherals, and lets users treat the remote resources to which they have access as if the resources were attached to their local machines.

Network Adapter Cards

Network adapter cards are used to handle high-speed data transfer between the CPU and the outside world, replacing parallel and serial ports for this purpose. Adapter cards usually plug into expansion slots inside each PC, though some network adapters are designed to plug into existing parallel ports.

The first function of an adapter card is to take the low-power electrical signals that come from the CPU and transform them into a more robust stream of bits that can be sent out into the hostile world in a serial fashion. An adapter may accept 8, 16, or 32 bits at a time (in parallel) from the CPU. Older 8086 and 8088 PCs are limited to 8-bit processing, so an 8-bit adapter is essential. PC AT-class machines running 80286 CPUs can accept either 8-bit or 16-bit adapters. An 80386 or 80486 PC can take advantage of a 32-bit adapter for very fast data transfer.

Input/Output Techniques Used by Network Adapters

The width of the adapter's connection to the PC is not the only factor that determines its speed. The *Input/Output (I/O) technique* used to move data between the board and the PC's RAM makes a big difference. There are four I/O techniques, and some PCs will not support all four, so most modern adapter cards allow you to select between at least two of the different methods. When you buy adapters, make sure they support the I/O technique(s) your PCs can use; these are briefly summarized as follows:

✦ *Programmed I/O* Programmed I/O is fast, uses little memory, and is preferred in most cases. It requires an 80286 or higher CPU. It requires active intervention from the CPU. This can cause "jerky" operation in multitasking situations. An 8-bit programmed I/O transfer is really slow.

✦ *Direct Memory Access (DMA)* DMA uses special chips, called Direct Memory Access Contollers, that perform transfers concurrently with CPU operation. Since it is 8-bit technology, a 16-bit word takes time to process and so is very slow by modern standards. Since data transfers are performed externally to the CPU's memory management logic, a multitasking operating system must be made aware of the presence of DMA devices. It is probably best to use DMA only with 8086 or 8088 CPUs.

✦ *Shared memory I/O* This is the fastest way to move data to and from the network adapter. Available in 8-bit and 16-bit versions, but 16-bit cards often run into memory conflicts with other devices. As with DMA, a multitasking operating system must be made aware of a shared-memory device. You get the advantages of DMA without the speed penalty. However you can expect a lot of timing problems, as the handshaking performed on the bus is quite involved. The devices are difficult to install in a PC containing VGA video or other memory-intensive devices.

✦ *Bus mastering* This is used primarily with MCA and EISA computers. It is very expensive and is best used only on computers that must frequently move large files.

Adapter IRQ Requirements

There are no standards for assigning interrupts to network adapters. Many adapter cards come from the factory set up to use IRQ3, which will always work if you have only one serial port installed. Even if you have a second serial port, it can share IRQ3 with the network adapter as long as the port and adapter are not used at the same time.

IRQ5 can often be used for a network adapter. PC-AT class machines only use this interrupt for second printer ports (LPT2) and tape drive controllers; if you have neither, IRQ5 should work for a network adapter. But do not use IRQ5 in a PC-XT equipped with a hard drive; the disk controller monopolizes IRQ5.

4

Other Useful Adapter Options

The majority of LAN adapters sold today include a socket for a *remote boot ROM*. This Read-Only Memory chip lets a workstation take its DOS boot files from a remote computer; that eliminates the need for any disk drives in the workstation! Diskless workstations eliminate the possibility of files being stolen. As you might expect, diskless stations cost less and are generally smaller than complete PCs.

Some minor niceties in adapter cards include an LED light to indicate when a card is receiving or sending data, and DIP switches that are exposed to the outside when the card is installed. The latter make it easy to reconfigure a card without opening the computer's case.

Network Protocols: ARCnet, Ethernet, and Token-Ring

So far, we have only dealt with what goes on between the CPU and the adapter card. (High-speed linking *does* get complicated!) There are two common standards for dealing with PC-to-PC LAN communications, called *network protocols*.

ARCnet Protocol   The *ARCnet* protocol is the older and slower of the two. ARCnet cards move data at a rated speed of 2.5 million bits per second (Mbps). Actual transmission speed is generally much lower, about 40 to 80 percent of rated speeds. The main advantage of ARCnet today is its low cost; adapters can readily be found for less than $100, sometimes as low as $35.

ARCnet can keep up with 8086, 8088, and even some slower 80286 computers in a small network of up to 100 users. But it makes no sense to hitch an 80386 or 80486 race horse to a plodding ARCnet LAN.

Ethernet Protocol   The *Ethernet* protocol can connect up to 1024 workstations. Its rated speed is 10 million bps, while actual speeds run about 2 to 4 Mbps. Ethernet is far more popular than ARCnet, and many more vendors support it. Prices for Ethernet boards can range from $150 to $250 when purchased separately from software. Novell bundles two Ethernet adapters with cable, connectors, and its NetWare Lite software for around $500.

Ethernet buyers may want to include attachment unit interface (AUI) ports in their adapter specifications. The AUI port connects to a *transceiver*, which can accept thick or thin Ethernet coaxial cable or fiber optic cable. Boards with AUI ports offer more flexibility when it comes to cabling options.

Token-Ring Protocol   The *Token-Ring* protocol is strongly championed by IBM, making it a good choice (though not the only one) if you need to link a LAN of PCs to an IBM mini- or mainframe environment. Early IBM Token-Ring adapters run at a rated speed of 4 Mbps; since 1989, Big Blue has been selling 16 Mbps Token-Ring hardware. A Token-Ring LAN is considerably more expensive than either ARCnet or Ethernet.

Cables: Coaxial, Twisted-Pair, and Fiber-Optic

Cables do more than just carry electricity in a LAN. Their electrical characteristics form an essential part of each different network protocol. This means you cannot use just any kind of cable that has the right number of wires in it. The network adapter you buy determines the kind(s) of cable you can use. The three different types of cables are shown in Figure 4-1.

Coaxial Cable

Coaxial cable is familiar to cable TV subscribers. Coax, as it is called, consists of a central wire, a layer of insulating plastic, another layer of woven copper, and an outer layer of insulation. The woven metal layer shields the central wire from outside electromagnetic interference and

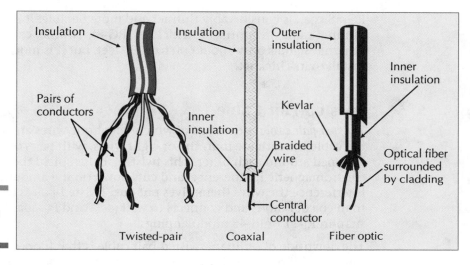

Three main
types of cable
Figure 4-1.

prevents the radiation generated by the data moving through the
central wire from interfering with nearby devices. Some types of coax
add a layer of metal foil on top of the woven layer to provide more
shielding.

NOTE: The distance between the central wire and its woven
shielding, the type of insulation used between them, and other
characteristics determine the *impedance* (a measure of electrical
resistance) of a coaxial cable. Impedance is measured in ohms and is
used to rate cables. The more resistance (higher impedance) a wire has,
the less far it can carry a signal before it fades. You cannot tell a cable's
impedance by its outer appearance, so industry standard codes are
generally imprinted every few inches on the outer sheath.

Ethernet uses coax cable designated RG-8 to carry signals up to 1640
feet. RG-8 coax is rather thick and stiff; the nickname "frozen yellow
garden hose" gives a good idea of what it is like to install RG-8 coax. It
is typically used to carry combined signals from several workstations
between floors in a building or building to building.

RG-58 coax is considerably thinner and more flexible. It is often called Thinnet cable, in contrast to Thicknet (RG-8). Thinnet can carry Ethernet signals only about 600 to 1000 feet, but it is much easier to install than Thicknet.

Twisted-Pair Cable

Twisted-pair cable is the stuff of which telephone wires are made. Inside the cable's sheath are four, six, or eight wires, with pairs of wires wrapped around each other. This twisting helps shield the wires from electromagnetic interference, and cuts down on the amount of interference the wires themselves put out. Twisted-pair is less expensive than coaxial cable, and connects to wall jacks and PC adapters using snap-in RJ-11 or RJ-45 modular plugs.

The downside of ordinary twisted-pair cable is that it does not provide much shielding. Some LAN vendors claim their twisted-pair wiring schemes can use existing idle phone wires in building walls, saving the cost and hassle of running new cable; most LAN experts, however, advise against it.

Shielded twisted-pair adds the woven or foil shield found in twisted-pair cable to the shielding effect of pair-twisting. IBM's Token-Ring protocol specifies this type of cable, which is also known as *data-grade twisted-pair*. Whatever you call it, it is more difficult to install than comparable coaxial cable, and more expensive.

Fiber-Optic Cable

Fiber-optic cable is made of glass fibers rather than wire. It uses light instead of electricity to carry data signals. The main advantages of fiber-optic cable over metal wires are distance and security. Fiber-optic cabling also has a huge bandwidth. You could plug a fiber line into your local cable TV feed, toss in your computer's network traffic, and still have room for a few thousand phone conversations.

Light does not lose signal strength anywhere near as rapidly as electrical signals, so fiber-optic links can carry data more than 11 times the maximum distance possible for coax, and 15 times farther than twisted-pair. Light is immune to electromagnetic interference from motors, fluorescent lights, and other sources that weaken electrical signals.

Electrical wires are easily tapped; if you can touch a coaxial LAN cable, you can siphon off any data moving through it. But since the only way to intercept fiber-optic signals is to cut the cable, it is impossible to tap fiber data streams without immediately alerting the network users.

Fiber is the most expensive cabling choice, about $2.00 per foot versus 10 to 12 cents for unshielded twisted-pair and 20 to 40 cents for coax. But people who need long-distance links, high reliability, and airtight security are choosing fiber; they include bankers, stockbrokers, medical technicians, and military personnel.

How LANs Shape Up: Star and Bus Topologies

A LAN's *physical topology* is the fundamental shape its cables describe as they run from PC to PC. The two types you will find on the market are the *star* and *bus* topologies; the latter is also known as a *daisy-chain* topology. Diagrams of the two topologies are shown in Figure 4-2.

A daisy-chain topology runs cable along the shortest path from one network node to the next, like a road running past a series of houses. Each node taps into the cable through a short T-connector, which may be visualized as the driveway connecting each house's garage to the street. ARCnet and Ethernet can use the daisy-chain topology; Token-Ring cannot.

A daisy-chain topology uses a minimal amount of cable to link a given number of nodes. On the downside, the electrical characteristics of this arrangement are such that any break in the cable will halt all traffic on the LAN.

The star topology is less vulnerable than a daisy chain. Each node is

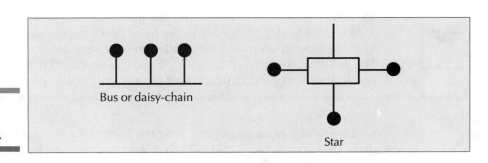

The two topologies
Figure 4-2.

linked to a central wiring hub. A break in one node's cable will knock it off the LAN, but the other links are unaffected. The star requires more cable and a wiring hub that may run $500 to $600 for eight connections. All three major protocols can use a star topology, though they use it in different ways.

Peer-to-Peer and Client/Server LANs

You need to decide which computer(s) on your LAN are going to provide the disk space and peripherals the others will use. When a computer fulfills a remote request for access to its disk, printer, modem, and so on, it is said to be acting as a *server*. The PC making the request is the server's *client*.

A *dedicated server* does nothing else but provide access to LAN resources for one or more clients. All shared resources— software, data files, printers, modems, and so on—are attached to the server. Client workstations need only satisfy local processing needs; they can be much smaller and cheaper than the server.

As you would expect, a server is generally a pretty high-powered and expensive machine, though at heart it is just another desktop computer. Servers require speedy processors, unusually fast and large hard drives, lots of RAM, and plenty of communications ports to handle a multitude of clients. A typical server for 100 to 200 clients might include an 80386 25MHz CPU, hard drive(s) holding hundreds of megabytes with average access times of 9 to 18 milliseconds, 4MB to 32MB of RAM, a math coprocessor, one or two high-speed printers, and perhaps a modem or CD-ROM drive. Such a PC system can cost over $10,000.

NOTE: A powerful server does not guarantee fast response over the LAN. Adapter cards may prove to be bottlenecks if a server has 10 or more clients; even a 10 Mbps adapter may keep some clients waiting. The solution is to install two or more adapter cards in the server and break the client group into smaller groups assigned to each adapter.

Smaller workgroups might not have the budget for an expensive dedicated server. LANs that get fairly light use may get by with a *nondedicated server*—a machine that can double as a local workstation while fulfilling client requests in the background. The key factor is not how many clients use the LAN, but how often the server must simultaneously handle remote and local tasks. Foreground tasks will noticeably slow down while the server handles client requests. The person using the local console to write a letter might not notice much slowdown, or may not use the local console very often. On the other hand, someone constantly recalculating large spreadsheets will not want their machine used as a LAN server.

The workload can be distributed among several computers on the LAN in what is called a *peer-to-peer network*. Each PC contributes some of its processing power and attached resources to the pool of disk space, printers, and so on that are available to the other members of the LAN. This arrangement spreads the work around, hopefully enabling every workstation to function without seriously slowing down foreground tasks. Peer-to-peer LANs often include "specialist" machines: file servers with large fast drives, print servers with lots of RAM for buffering, communications servers with modems and fax boards, and so on.

Client/server LANs are great if you can afford a dedicated high-powered PC. It is much easier to monitor and manage network resources if they are all in one place. Users will not suffer any slowdowns due to remote access of their workstations. A dedicated server can be optimized for speed and power, while workstations can be less expensive 80286 or even 8086/8088 computers.

The downside of client/server arrangements is that all your eggs go into one basket. If the server crashes or must be taken offline, everyone's work will be affected. If you plan a single-server LAN, buy the most reliable equipment you can afford, maintain it well, and make daily backup copies of all critical data. It is an excellent idea to have a spare PC around, in case the server dies, or arrange with a dealer to get one within hours if needed.

LAN Operating Software

The software that manages data traffic, determines what resources are available to clients, and makes remote resources virtual devices, is called the *Network Operating System,* or NOS. PAIRSHARE is a shareware example of a NOS. Novell, Inc., is undeniably the leader in NOS software, with its NetWare line of products. LANtastic (Artisoft, Inc.), is very popular for networks of up to 100 users.

Microsoft's new Windows for Workgroups makes peer-to-peer networking available to the masses. Microsoft Corporation is also pushing strongly and successfully for its LAN Manager NOS, which has the advantage of very broad support among computer vendors. Version 2.0 of LAN Manager requires the OS/2 operating system on servers, while client workstations can use OS/2 or other operating systems. LAN Manager 2.0 is an important recent development in network operating systems, because it is designed from scratch to handle the multitasking chores of a server. When Windows NT hits the market, LAN Manager will be available on that platform as well, which should give Microsoft a strong position in the multitasking operating system arena.

Banyan Systems' VINES (VIrtual NEtworking Software) takes its flavor from the UNIX operating system developed by AT&T. VINES is known for its ability to link widely separated file servers over long-distance telecommunications lines. Another VINES innovation that has been copied by Novell and Microsoft is called global naming services, a convenient way of naming resources and users on various servers and nodes across a network. The LAN administrator does not have to sit down at each server to configure resources and user rights; one step from one server does it all.

Where To Learn More About LANs

This whirlwind tour of local area networking is only intended to point in the right direction and give a gentle nudge to get you started. Volumes have been written on each of the topics discussed in the preceding paragraphs. There are a number of magazines that specialize in the networking arena. *LAN TIMES* is one that would appeal to readers who feel comfortable with this book.

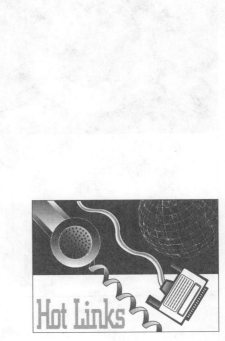

CHAPTER

Hot Links

5

LONG-DISTANCE LINKING: MODEMS AND ONLINE SERVICES

The world's largest network, without doubt, is the global telephone system. Through its uncountable miles of wire it can link virtually any point on the earth to any other. Where wire doesn't reach, radio beams carried by satellites do.

Telephone lines can carry data as well as voice signals; all you need is a modem, a device that translates between the weak digital electrical signals generated by a computer and the robust, analog signals carried by telephone lines. With a modem, you can link your PC to any other computer on the planet, permanently or for any period of time.

NOTE: The word "modem" stands for MOdulate/DEModulate. The modem *modulates* the digital computer signal to an analog signal, which runs along the telephone system and is *demodulated* by the receiving modem back into the digital signal that the receiving computer can understand.

Permanent modem links are portions of the telephone network leased from the phone company for your exclusive use; they are called *dedicated lines* or *leased lines*. Leased lines cost a bundle; a 1000-mile stretch that is certified to carry data at 1.544 Mbps can cost $11,000 per month! Even faster lines (up to 45 Mbps) can be leased for even more outrageous fees—over $100,000 per month.

This chapter focuses on more affordable *dial-up lines,* the kind you already use at home, at work, and anywhere else when you want to "reach out and touch someone."

What Dial-Up Modems Can Do

Dial-up modem links use serial communications, either asynchronous or synchronous (see Chapter 1 for details of sync and async communications). Dial-up connections, because they may extend so far and through so many data-hostile environments, are relatively slow, even by serial port standards. About two-thirds of the dial-up modems in use today chug along at 2400 bps or less. Most of the other one-third can do 9600 bps. The most expensive dial-up modems can reach 14,400 bps. The top speed for dial-up links is 19,200 bps.

Modern modems use data-compression algorithms to compensate for their relatively slow transfer speeds, and error-correcting protocols to compensate for the high line-noise levels common in dial-up links. Error-correction and data compression vastly improve the usefulness of modems, but also complicate buying decisions and making connections to unfamiliar remote computers.

Modem links can be used much like zero-slot LANs to control file transfer, and exchange electronic mail. *Remote-control software* lets you dial up another computer and operate it as if you were sitting in front of its keyboard instead of your own. *Fax modems* can send files directly from your disk to any fax machine in the world, without printing the document and running it through a scanner. Fax modems can also receive inbound faxes and store them on a disk as graphics files.

Features to Look for in a Modem

When shopping for a modem, you need to consider several aspects of its construction and built-in features:

5

+ Do you want an internal modem that plugs into an expansion slot in your PC, or an external model that occupies a separate box on your desk?

+ The speed you need depends on the uses to which you will put your modem; 2400 bps is good enough for interactive uses, like online database searching, and costs much less than 9600 or 14,400 bps.

+ Error-correction protocols are essential if you plan to use synchronous communications to transfer files. But asynchronous communication is actually slowed down by error correction.

+ Data compression can double or quadruple the amount of information your modem transmits at any given speed, but only when you are sending uncompressed files to another modem equipped with the same data-compression algorithm as your own.

The price of a modem is directly related to these feature decisions. The following sections discuss the pros and cons of each type of feature and the relative cost of adding features to your modem.

Internal Versus External Modems

An internal modem generally costs $20 to $50 less than the same modem in an external case. External modems also require serial cables to connect them to your PC; many vendors do not include cables. External modems easily plug into existing serial port connectors, without removing the computer's cover. Internal modems include serial port circuitry that must be configured to an open COM port address and IRQ address. External modems have front-panel displays that let you monitor the modem's operation, the progress of a call, and even the actual speed of a given connection. Internal modems do not provide visual feedback but there is software that will give you that feedback. Finally, external modems are a bit more flexible in that they are bus independent, so if your system dies and you change to a different kind of computer (say a Mac), you can still use your modem.

Connect Speed Ratings: CCITT v.22, v.22bis, v.32, and v.32bis

The highest speed a modem can achieve over a dial-up line is the most significant factor influencing its price. Reliable 2400 bps modems cost between $50 and $150, while 9600 bps models range from about $250 to over $1,200, and 14,400 bps modems start at about $400.

A 2400 bps modem takes over 80 minutes to transfer 1.2MB of data, the capacity of a 5 1/4-inch high-density disk. A 9600 bps modem would require only about 21 minutes, and a 14,400 bps modem would do the job in under 15 minutes. If you often transfer large files at long-distance carrier prices, a high-speed modem is well worth the extra cost.

Some vendors grossly misrepresent their products' speed capabilities, by advertising the higher "effective throughput speed" provided by data-compression algorithms. Data-compression effectiveness varies depending on the type of data being transmitted, whether it is already compressed, and whether the remote modem uses the same data-compression method.

Fortunately, most modems adhere to certain international standards that define how fast they transfer data from modem to modem. Look for these CCITT (Consultative Committee for International Telephony and Telegraphy) designations when comparing modem speeds:

Speed	CCITT Standard
1200 bps	v.22
2400 bps	v.22bis
9600 bps	v.32
14,400 bps	v.32bis

NOTE: "bis" indicates an enhanced version of an earlier standard.

Each higher-speed standard is able to slow down to match modems with lower maximum speeds or to compensate for excessive line noise. Examine these CCITT ratings rather than the vendor's advertising copy to determine the most important and consistent speed you can expect.

The CCITT v.*XX* standards are nearly universal, but you might run into some proprietary high-speed protocols, such as Telebit's PEP (Packetized Ensemble Protocol) and U. S. Robotics' HST (High Speed Technology) protocol. Be aware that such modems will only communicate at high speeds with identical modems from the same vendor. Most vendors are switching to CCITT standards, or at least offering both CCITT and their proprietary protocols in the same modem. You can expect proprietary protocols to disappear over the next two years.

Error-Correction Protocols: MNP 1 Through 4 and CCITT v.42

Dial-up telephone lines are designed to carry voice signals, which do not require the precision of data transmission. What sounds like a mildly annoying hiss when you talk to Grandma can be totally catastrophic to a modem file transfer. *Line noise* is electromagnetic interference that can corrupt bits in a data stream. A few bad bits may show up as garbage characters in a text file, but the text is often still readable. However, a single altered bit in a binary file such as an executable program can render the whole file useless, if not downright dangerous to run on your computer. Line noise can also cause modems to lose the *carrier signal* that tells them they are connected to each other, a very frustrating experience for the user.

Modems can be purchased with error-correcting protocols built into them; the additional cost is only about $20 to $30 versus a non-error-correcting version of the same modem. When two modems establish an error-corrected connection, the data you send to your modem is guaranteed to emerge from the other modem unchanged.

Error-correcting protocols built into modems are called *hardware-based error-correction*; do not confuse them with the file-transfer protocols often found in the terminal-emulation software you use to communicate with your modem. Some file-transfer protocols, notably Ymodem-G, can be used *only* with hardware-based error-correction modems. Other file-transfer protocols duplicate the efforts of hardware-based error correction, and can slow down data-transfer speed.

The Microcom Networking Protocol (MNP) was the first hardware-based error-correction scheme to achieve widespread use, beginning in the mid-1980s. MNP has evolved through several levels of sophistication; most modern error-correcting modems incorporate MNP Levels 1 through 4.

The CCITT v.42 standard for hardware-based error-correction incorporates MNP Levels 1 through 4 as an alternative protocol so that CCITT-compliant modems can also communicate error free with MNP-only modems.

Error correction is a great convenience under the best line conditions. It is sorely needed in areas where line noise frequently disrupts modem communications, or when calling very long distances.

Data Compression: MNP 5 and 7, CCITT v.42bis

Anyone who has received a program *archived* with a utility like ARC or ZIP, or who uses "disk doubling" software such as Stacker to increase a hard drive's capacity, is familiar with data compression. *Data compression* is a way of describing information using fewer bits than the original data format used; think of it as shorthand for data files. Reversing the compression process restores the data to its original format so standard application software can read it.

A modem equipped with data-compression algorithms can accept uncompressed data from your PC *faster* than the modem can transmit data to another modem. Normal English text files can often be compressed to one-fourth their original size, so a 2400 bps modem can accept text from your PC at a rate of $4 \times 2400 = 9600$ bps. It looks to you as if you are transferring data at 9600 bps. A 9600 bps modem can accept input at up to $4 \times 9600 = 38,400$ bps. A 14,400 bps modem can appear to be moving data at 57,600 bps, and indeed it is—from your PC to the modem.

But data travels from modem to modem at the highest connect speed the modems can negotiate: 2400, 9600, 14,400, and so on. Do not be confused by vendors who claim to be selling 38,400 baud modems; there is no such thing.

Data compression is generally useful, but actual throughput is almost always less than the theoretical maximums described above. Binary files compress far less than text files, so you lose some of the apparent speed gain when moving programs around. Archive files compressed with PKZIP, ARC, LHARC, and other stand-alone utilities may actually *expand* when run through a modem's compression algorithms! In any case, it is counterproductive to recompress an already compressed file; the time spent analyzing the file slows down the data-transfer rate to no purpose.

Microcom Corp. developed the first modem data-compression protocol, calling it MNP Level 5. MNP 5 can compress English text files to about half their original size, effectively doubling the throughput rate of a modem. Many 2400 bps modem vendors therefore advertise 4800 bps capabilities using MNP 5. What they don't tell you is that the receiving modem must also be equipped with MNP 5 or the file will not be compressed at all.

The CCITT v.42bis data-compression protocol, like v.42 error correction, incorporates its MNP equivalent to provide wider compatibility with other modems. The v.42bis modems can compress files to one-quarter their original size, equivalent to a 400 percent increase in effective data throughput. Another advantage of v.42bis is that it does not try to compress a file unless a quick analysis indicates that effective throughput would be increased; v.42bis leaves archived files alone and does not try to compress them further.

Data compression is worth its minimal extra cost if you transfer uncompressed files, or if you use your modem primarily in an interactive mode, where much of the data going back and forth consists of text screens.

Software for Using Modems

After you buy a modem and install it, you still need to add software to accomplish anything. There are three general categories of communications software for modems:

✦ *Terminal-emulation programs* let your computer call another via modem and interact with it.

✦ *Remote-control programs* let your computer take control of (or be controlled by) another computer through a phone line.

✦ *Bulletin board systems* let your computer act as a central communication and resource center for any number of users.

Most people will never use remote control or host software, but every modem owner should know as much as possible about terminal-emulation programs. A modem without terminal emulation is like a monitor without a keyboard.

Terminal-Emulation Program Features

The basic purpose of terminal software is to let you type on your keyboard and have what you type sent to the serial port, which in turn passes data to the modem. Your modem then transmits data to the remote modem, which passes it to its computer via another serial port. The remote computer's responses to the data you send (if any) come back to your computer via the same route and are commonly displayed on your monitor.

Originally, data terminals were not computers, just circuitry that made them effectively no more than keyboards and screens. The standards by which people communicate with remote computers were developed using these *dumb terminals,* so modern PCs must emulate, or mimic, the ways in which dumb terminals operate. The power of a personal computer, however, permits additional functions that dumb terminals could never accomplish; you will learn about some of these functions later in this chapter.

Examples of terminal-emulation software for IBM PCs include ProComm Plus (Datastorm Technologies), Telix (Exis, Inc.), Qmodem (Mustang Software), Crosstalk (Digital Communications Associates), and Smartcom (Hayes Microcomputer Products). Macintosh owners often use White Knight, Red Ryder, or Zterm terminal software. There are hundreds of terminal-emulation programs on the market, most of them distributed as shareware via bulletin board systems and disk vendors.

When shopping for terminal-emulation software, you should consider the following features:

✦ *COM port support* The software must be set to use the COM port and IRQ to which your modem is configured. Obsolete terminal programs do not support COM3 or COM4. Surprisingly, neither did the original version of Windows 3.0, so you should make sure which ports a program supports before you buy it, no matter how recent its vintage.

✦ *Terminal-emulation types* If you will be communicating with a computer that requires a specific type of terminal, be sure the emulation software you buy can emulate that terminal. Most terminal programs come with a variety of terminal-emulation types, ranging from generic TTY (teletype printer) emulation that will work at some basic level with almost any computer, to highly specific and relatively rare specimens like the Wyse Model 50 data terminal. Any terminal software intended for general use should include at least TTY, ANSI-BBS, and DEC VT100 terminal types.

✦ *File-transfer protocols* Sending (uploading) and retrieving (downloading) files is the most common use for terminal software. The rules for this game of toss-and-catch are called *file-transfer protocols*. It is essential that both computers use the same protocols when transferring files; otherwise, it would be as if a pitcher threw a high fast ball while the catcher was expecting a low outside curve. You need a terminal program that supports ASCII, Xmodem, Ymodem, Kermit, and Zmodem file-transfer protocols. This suite of protocols will almost always provide at least one match with the protocols on any machine to which you connect.

✦ *Dialing directory* A *dialing directory* is essentially a database file whose records consist of the parameters peculiar to each remote computer you regularly call: its name, phone number, communications settings, file-transfer protocol, your password, and so on. Dialing directories should have basic text-string search capabilities, so you can type in a few letters from the name of a system and call up its record, ready to be dialed, with a single keystroke.

✦ *Disk capture/logging* You should be able to record everything that passes across your screen during a session with a remote computer

5

to a file on your hard drive, called a *log file* or *capture file.* Logging can save a lot of connect time charges by letting messages scroll down the screen and into the log file much faster than you could read them while connected. After hanging up, you can use any text editor or viewing utility to read the log file.

✦ *Script recording/programming* A *script* is a set of instructions your terminal software executes whenever it dials the remote system for which the script was created. Scripts allow you to automate many routine procedures, such as entering your user name and password, checking your mailbox, downloading a list of files uploaded since you last logged on, capturing new information bulletins, and logging off automatically. Many terminal programs have a learn-script or record-script mode; every response you make to prompts from the remote host are saved in a script file, so you can repeat the same sequence of responses later with just one keystroke. More sophisticated scripts can be written like programs. Programmed scripts can use IF...THEN...ELSE commands to handle unexpected responses from the remote computer (such as a sudden loss of carrier), and even be set to automatically call a remote system, execute a script, and log off when you are not around.

Remote-Control Software

Terminal-emulation software focuses on exchanges of messages and files. Remote-control software has a different emphasis: it run programs on a remote computer as if you were sitting at its keyboard. Some examples of remote-control software include CloseUp from Norton-Lambert, PC Anywhere from DMA, Remote by DCA, and Carbon Copy from MicroCom.

One of the most popular uses of remote-control software is to collect e-mail from a remote location. Remote-control (RC) software is often used by customer service reps to troubleshoot customer problems over the phone. An RC program's *host module,* the portion that receives inbound calls, can be installed over a phone line with the remote customer's cooperation. Usually, all the customer need do is type two or three DOS commands to set up the serial port and modem to receive the RC software. Once the RC program is installed, the customer service rep can observe how the host computer behaves as the customer tries to repeat the steps that led to the problem. It is like standing over someone's shoulder while they use their computer, but much cheaper than flying to a customer's location.

RC programs are also handy for people who take work home with them. If you need some data you didn't bring with you, just dial up your office PC, extract the needed records from a spreadsheet, database, or whatever, and download them to your home computer. You can pick up or transmit electronic mail, even access other computers on a LAN, just as if you were at the office.

Bulletin Board Systems

Remote-control software establishes a temporary user-to-computer link. Local area networks provide permanent links between many users. People use LANs to communicate with each other, not just to use each other's computing resources. Bulletin board systems (BBS for short) combine the convenience and flexibility of dial-up remote control and the benefits of sharing resources (human as well as digital) with a community of users. Bulletin boards can range from small special-interest boards to giant online services like CompuServe, MCI, and Prodigy, which connect thousands of users to one another and to "the intellects of the world."

A BBS is a modem-equipped computer that is generally left ready to accept incoming calls 24 hours a day. The BBS *sysop* (SYStem OPerator) can precisely control what callers can do once they connect, how long they can remain connected, and even whose calls will be accepted by the BBS.

BBS software is designed to facilitate interaction between people, not merely between computers. The origin and evolution of BBS software clearly illustrate this focus on person-to-person interaction. Ward Christensen decided in 1978 to put the messages and bulletins found on his computer club's cork bulletin board on a modem-equipped computer, so that members could post and read club-related information without coming to the club's headquarters. Instead, they would call Christensen's computer using terminal software, peruse a short list of message subjects, select the items they wanted to read in full, and reply if they wanted.

The exchange of messages was the important thing; that messages were posted on a computer instead of a cork bulletin board was merely a convenience. But what a convenience it was!

Club members soon prevailed upon Christensen to add file-exchange capabilities to his computer bulletin board, so they could swap programs they had written. This second step in BBS evolution was like the first, in that the significant interaction was between people, not between a person and the computer running the BBS software.

Eventually, remote control functions were added to BBS software, creating a class of BBS features that emphasize the user-to-computer relationship. Today, you can play a game on a BBS, perform complex calculations or database searches, even "drop to DOS" and take over remote control of the BBS computer and its attached resources.

The basic functions of BBS software can be summarized as follows:

+ *Messaging* Private electronic mail can be addressed to specific users, or messages can be posted in public forums where all later callers can read and answer them.

+ *Teleconferencing* In a multiline BBS, callers on two or more different phone lines can type messages to each other in real time, conducting a conversation via their keyboards. This kind of chat on a one-line BBS is limited to the current caller and the sysop.

+ *File exchange* Callers can upload (send) files to a BBS, which stores them on its hard drive(s). Callers can enter descriptions of their uploads, for example, "World's best lottery number picker." Then later callers can search the file of descriptions and download files they want. Many BBS also offer private, person-to-person file exchanges.

+ *Remote processing* Callers can run software that resides on the BBSs' hard drives, using the BBSs' processing power instead of their own computers.

Uses for Bulletin Board Systems

There are an estimated 50,000 bulletin board systems in the United States that are open to the public.

Hobbyist or Nonprofit Boards

Many of these may be hobbyist or public service systems in which profit is not the goal; some examples include

+ *The National Cave Divers' Association BBS*, where members buy, sell, and swap equipment; organize dive trips; discuss the finer points of their sport; trade graphics files containing photographs of their favorite haunts; and so on.

+ *The Big Sky Telegraph* network of Apple computers in over 20 Montana rural elementary schools. The BBS provides a focal point for exchange of educational software, classroom notes, community bulletins, and students' messages.

+ *The Washington State Department of Trade BBS*, a system sponsored by the government, provides announcements of state contracts available for bid, economic development and small-business assistance resources, and even a database in which corporate buyers can search for minority and small-business suppliers.

+ *The Dante Project BBS* at Dartmouth University, where scholars all over the world can peruse 600 years' worth of commentaries on Dante's Comedia Inferno and other writings.

Commercial Boards

There are a growing number of commercial ventures that sell BBS services to the general public. A BBS can be started with less than $1,000, making "infopreneuring" one of the most affordable and potentially lucrative business opportunities. Prodigy, CompuServe, and other commercial online services differ from BBSs primarily in size, not in the capabilities they offer. Some examples of successful commercial BBSs include

+ *EXEC-PC*, started by Bob Mahoney with just one line, a 20MB hard drive, and a PC-XT over ten years ago. Today Mahoney's system has 250 lines handling more than 5000 calls per day. A one-year membership costs $60. With more than 10,000 members, this bootstrap business is doing just fine, thank you.

◆ *Computer Discount BBS*, a subsidiary of a Florida computer reseller, offers hardware and software by modem. Search for the product you want by vendor, product type, or model. Enter your Visa or MasterCard number, and it ships the next day. With no sales staff or manual data entry, this system sells over $1,000,000 per year.

◆ *The Lifestyle BBS*, unabashedly devoted to computer sex. No matter how rare the kink in your libido may be, you will probably find a kindred soul in Lifestyle's membership database. Then it is a simple matter to exchange e-mail, engage in some live chat, swap pictures, even arrange a meeting if you wish. This virtual swingers' club grew from a single-line BBS to more than 50 lines and 1000 calls per day in its first year. The sysop charges by the minute, like 1-900 chat services.

Corporate Boards

Another 100,000 private BBSs are maintained by businesses exclusively for their employees and/or customers. That corporations have so strongly adopted what started out as a hobbyist phenomenon is an indication of how valuable a BBS can be. Some applications and examples of private BBSs include

◆ *Customer support* Microsoft Corp., WordPerfect Corp., IBM, Hewlett-Packard, Dell Computer Corp., Western Digital Corp., and hundreds of other hardware/software makers maintain BBSs for their customers. Solutions to common technical problems, software upgrades, and third-party add-on utilities are posted where customers can get them any time of the day or week. Messages about nonurgent technical questions can be left for tech support reps, and the answers downloaded verbatim instead of hastily and incompletely copied by phone. Many of these companies have reaped an unexpected benefit: callers solve each other's problems, relieving some of the burden on the company's staff!

◆ *Remote data access* Field auditors and consultants for Arthur Anderson & Co. can log into the firm's extensive databases of federal and state tax laws, regulations, and court decisions. They can also send and receive private e-mail concerning confidential client matters without going through commercial e-mail services.

✦ *Remote data collection* HoneyBaked Hams store managers nationwide upload their daily sales and inventory data to the company's headquarters within minutes of closing time each day. Current, precise information helps the firm plan its production and delivery schedules better. Arby's Roast Beef and Mrs. Field's Cookies have similar systems.

These are just a few examples of BBS applications. Dozens more are cropping up every day: environmental databanks, employment services, audio compact disks, satellite weather maps, flowers, office supplies, used video game cartridges—you name it, and someone is probably running a BBS devoted to it.

5

BBS Software

You don't need BBS software to log on to an existing BBS, but you can use BBS software to start up a bulletin board of your own, to connect up friends with like interests, for example, or to keep in touch with your far-flung family.

There are dozens of BBS software packages, most of them shareware programs developed by hobbyists for their own use and later distributed on the honor system: try the software and send the author a registration fee if you like it. RBBS, one of the oldest packages, is a public-domain program; no registration fee is required. Most shareware BBS programs will cost less than $100 to register; with registration comes technical support and upgrades—provided the shareware author sticks with his product. Many do not.

Commercial BBS software for IBM compatibles includes PCBoard (Clark Development Co.), WildCat! (Mustang Software, Inc.), The Major BBS (Galacticomm, Inc.), and TBBS (eSoft, Inc.). These are by no means the only commercial BBS software vendors, but they probably account for over 90 percent of commercial installations. You will find their addresses in Appendix E, "Resource Directory."

If you plan a one-line hobby BBS, just about any of the shareware programs will do. Commercial ventures should be supported by commercial vendors; you don't want your business to be your supplier's hobby. Commercial one-line software ranges in price from about $130 to $300, not much more than some shareware.

There are two types of BBS software: *single-node* packages, designed to run one phone line per PC, and *multinode* systems, which can service up to 64 lines from a single PC. PCBoard and WildCat! are examples of single-line software, while TBBS and The Major are multiline programs.

Multiple copies of single-node software can be run on a single PC under multitasking programs such as DESQview; this allows one PC to host several lines. A number of PCs can be linked by a LAN, and the BBS software can let one user on each PC communicate with users on other nodes.

Single-node software and multiple PCs have two advantages over multinode software running on a single PC:

1. If one PC's hard drive crashes, only the phone line(s) served by that computer go offline; if anything breaks in a multinode BBS' PC, you are temporarily out of business.
2. You can run external programs of just about any kind under a single-node BBS, much as you could run WordPerfect using remote-control software. Multiline software cannot run external programs, though TBBS and The Major both permit custom-written software to be merged with the BBS code.

Multinode BBS software has its own advantages:

✦ *Simplicity* The more layers of hardware and software you add to any system, the more time you will spend troubleshooting and replacing broken parts. Running multiple copies of a program under DesqView adds one layer of complexity; link several such PCs over a LAN and you will vastly complicate system maintenance.

✦ *Cost* Each additional phone line in a single-node BBS requires its own licensed copy of the BBS software. If you want to run more than four lines, you need at least two PCs, two network adapters, LAN software, and LAN cables. The total cost of a multinode BBS running four or more lines is generally less than the cost of a single-node BBS of the same size.

Summary: Modems Link You to the World

Mastering modems gives you total linking freedom; the entire universe of electronic information becomes literally a phone call away. Remote-control software can free you from offices and travel, and a BBS can bring the world to you.

5

CHAPTER

Hot Links

6 LINKING LAPTOP COMPUTERS AT HOME AND ON THE ROAD

Computing power used to be locked up in a climate-controlled room at corporate headquarters, zealously guarded by mysterious, aloof high priests of information. Personal computers let the cat out of the bag, and soon users truthfully couldn't bear to part with their PCs. Now computers go wherever their masters go.

The first attempts at portable computers were almost as big and heavy as their deskbound immediate ancestors. A 28-pound, suitcase-sized box qualifies as "portable" only by the most masochistic standards. Most of these monsters would not fit under an airline seat. Early portables had no battery packs, limiting their luggability to trips between electrical outlets.

Arm-weary traveling computerists were rescued by the advent of true *laptop computers,* which can be recognized by the following characteristics:

✦ Laptops sport at least a full 640K of main memory; they can run full-fledged software.

✦ They include keyboards with full-sized keys, not the rubbery little buttons generally called "chiclet keys."

✦ They can run off batteries as well as A/C power.

✦ They do not cause one's legs to fall asleep while writing a letter.

✦ Most laptops and their battery packs are just a bit too big to fit in a briefcase, which has given rise to an entire industry of laptop carry-all bags.

Notebook computers are a subspecies of laptops, with the preceding characteristics crammed into a still smaller package. Notebooks generally take less power than laptops, run longer on batteries, and actually fit in a standard briefcase with room to spare. When we talk about laptops, we include notebooks in the term.

Modern laptops can be loaded up with all the options of their desktop brethren: VGA screens, math coprocessors, mice, megabytes of RAM, and astoundingly small, high-capacity hard drives. Except for their necessarily cramped keyboards and comparatively small display screens, laptops demand no sacrifices in exchange for true go-anywhere computing power.

Laptop owners quickly realize that freedom can be a lonely condition. It is liberating to sever the wires chaining you to your desk, but sooner or later most people need a link to their office computers. Data collected in the field must often be transferred to office systems; the sooner the better for time-sensitive data collection such as sales orders. Even today's capacious laptop hard drives cannot hold every bit of data a user might need on the road, and invariably one forgets to pack exactly what one needs.

This chapter examines several linking options for laptop road warriors, including the following:

✦ Loading data into your laptop before leaving the office and unpacking data to your office machine(s) upon returning

✦ Using your laptop as a secondary resource for your desktop machine

✦ Linking to your office PC via modem, a task complicated by hotel and office telephone systems that were never designed for modems

✦ Linking a laptop to a LAN or mainframe computer

✦ Wireless links that preserve your laptop's mobility

Laptop connectivity is at an imperfect stage. You *can* link a laptop to just about anything, from just about anywhere. Whether a particular solution is worth the expense, trouble, and aggravation of often mediocre performance depends on how badly you need it.

Linking Laptop to Desktop at the Office

The easiest and most commonly needed laptop link is used to transfer files between a desktop machine and a laptop. If the two machines have compatible floppy drives, it is easy to copy a few files at a time between the two computers. But there are still quite a few desktop machines equipped only with 5 1/4-inch floppies, and most modern laptops take only 3 1/2-inch disks.

File Exchange Over Cables

Serial- or parallel-port file exchange is the solution to drive incompatibilities. LapLink was developed for this very purpose. A few very early and short-lived laptops omitted ports to save space; if you buy such a machine (at a flea market?), your only option is to install a compatible drive in the desktop computer.

Users are often hurrying to appointments or airports when they copy files from desktop to laptop. It is all too easy to copy the wrong files or leave some behind on the desktop machine. LapLink and other file-exchange software makes packing your laptop for a trip quick and foolproof. You can synchronize the files on the two machines in one operation, ensuring that you take with you all the latest versions of files you will need. If you frequently must update a particular set of files on both laptop and desktop, you can record the appropriate filenames, directory paths, and copying instructions once and then execute them at any time with the push of a button.

Sharing a Laptop's Disk with a Desktop PC

You can keep your laptop's files constantly up to date, and increase your desktop PC's storage capacity using disk-sharing solutions like Desk Connect, one of the programs included with this book. Desk Connect and a serial cable make your laptop's hard drive a virtual drive for your desktop machine.

A virtual drive, as you may recall from reading Chapter 4, is a disk drive on a remote PC that can be used as if it were attached to your local machine. If your desktop PC has drives A, B, and C, Desk Connect will assign drive letter D to your laptop's hard drive. You can then store, edit, copy, and delete files on the laptop exactly as if they were on your desktop's drives. You will *not* be able to execute programs stored on the laptop. Desk Connect offers remote access, but not remote execution capabilities. (PairWeb, for instance, will let you execute remote software across a serial port link.)

It makes sense to put your laptop to work at the office. The files you will need on the road can be kept constantly up to date, so all you need to do is unplug the serial cable and head for the door. The effective increase of available storage space for your desktop machine is another benefit of this solution.

Desk Connect turns your laptop into a server, totally dedicated to providing disk access to your desktop computer. You will not be able to use the laptop for anything else while Desk Connect is loaded. Accessing the laptop's drive will be noticeably slower than accessing your desktop drive, thanks to the relatively low speed of serial communications.

Docking Stations Convert Laptops to Desktops

Laptops have some major drawbacks: small displays, cramped keyboards, lack of upgradability, and few expansion options. Some laptop owners (about 17 percent) have overcome these problems and chucked their desktop machines altogether. *Docking stations* are expansion chassis that provide links to expansion slots, additional parallel and serial ports, floppy drives, external hard drives, expanded keyboards, and the other amenities for which there is no room in a laptop.

When a laptop comes home to roost, a special connector on its back plugs into a receptacle in the docking station. When it is time to hit the road, the laptop disconnects from its docking station while remaining a fully functional computer.

Today there are no universal docking stations that can accommodate several vendors' laptops; you must buy both components from the same vendor. Popular laptop/docking-station combos include Compaq Computer Corp.'s LTE 386s/20 and Desktop Expansion Base; Epson America Inc.'s NB3s and Expansion Unit; and Toshiba America Information Systems, Inc.'s T2000SX and Desk Station II.

The lack of a standard for laptop/docking station connections keeps prices high (around $1,000, in addition to the laptop) and users wary. Vendors recognize this problem and may well agree on a docking station standard in the next couple of years.

LANs and Laptops

A high-speed LAN link requires a network adapter (see Chapter 4). A desktop PC has internal expansion slots to accommodate such add ons. A laptop may have no slots, or nonstandard minislots. Even if you have an expansion slot in your laptop, you will need an adapter card made specifically to fit your brand and model.

A built-in LAN adapter is no use when you are away from the office and its LAN cables; it just makes your laptop heavier and drains the battery faster. Many laptop users opt instead for *pocket LAN adapters* that plug into a laptop's parallel port. These devices can be kept in a desk drawer or travel kit until needed. They are not as fast as cards, but adequate for most laptop-to-LAN needs.

File-exchange software can provide limited access to a LAN. You can connect your laptop to a PC, which in turn is linked to a LAN, and gain access to any virtual drives the second PC can access. LapLink and other software that can establish a file-exchange link via modem can also provide remote access to a LAN.

UDS Motorola's LanFast modem has a built-in network adapter, so it can be directly connected to a LAN instead of to a server. Remote computers, including laptops, can use this modem to access LAN resources. The LanFast modem, like others of its type, includes security features to prevent unauthorized callers from raiding the LAN. The modem can be set to allow access only after a recognized password is entered. A feature called *automated callback* prevents all calls except those from specific phone numbers from getting into the LAN; the modem hangs up after a password is entered, looks up a phone number associated with that password, and dials the caller's number. If the call came from another site, the caller won't get into the network.

Staying Connected While Traveling

Modems were made for laptops, but using a modem on the road can be difficult. Many hotels offer no way to plug an RJ-11 jack into a modem. PBX systems in offices you visit may require selecting an outbound line by pushing a button; modems don't have fingers. Staying connected can require intrepid ingenuity.

Phones in hotel rooms often lack RJ-11 modular plugs; they are permanently wired to their wall outlets to discourage theft. One way to jump this hurdle is to carry a piece of RJ-11 wire with a plug on only one end. The other end should have two alligator clips, attached to the innermost pair of wires in the cable. These two inner wires are almost always red and green (think Christmas!). Unscrew the mouthpiece of the phone, and you will see two contacts attaching to the microphone inside. Attach one of your alligator clips to each of these contacts, and plug the RJ-11 end into your modem. You will probably have to add a 9 and a pause command to the phone number you want your modem to dial so it can get an outside line.

If disassembling hotel property bothers you, try using an *acoustic coupler.* These venerable devices consist of a pair of soft rubber cups that cradle a telephone handset, covering both mouthpiece and earpiece, and circuitry that translates sound into electrical signals your modem can use. They don't work well at 2400 bps, and not at all at higher speeds.

Laptop modems, like LAN adapters, can be had as internal cards or pocket-sized external models. An external modem will work with any serial port (including a desktop PC's), while most cards are designed for specific laptop models. Pocket modems can be had for under $100, while internal machine-specific cards can cost $200 or more.

Wireless modems provide the ultimate in laptop liberty; see Chapter 9 to learn about these and other wireless linking options. Brace yourself for sticker shock; wireless modems routinely cost over $1,000. You will also pay for the cellular or packet-radio time you use.

Do Laptops Offer Freedom or Just Longer Chains?

6

"With freedom comes responsibility." That phrase was probably coined by someone's employer (or parent). Desktop computers were supposed to help people get work done faster so they could enjoy more leisure time; quite the opposite has occurred. The more work you can get done, the more you are expected to do.

You could not take work home while your computer was tied to a desk; now it can follow you anywhere. Workaholics and slavedrivers welcome the laptop linking revolution; should you?

CHAPTER

Hot Links

7

LINKING DOS-BASED PCS AND MACINTOSHES

The microcomputer world has two major standards—the DOS-based IBM-compatible (PC) and the Apple Macintosh (Mac). If you work in a large company, the chances are good that you deal with a mixture of PCs and Macs. If you've decided on a PC or a Mac as your favorite platform, don't think that you must cut yourself off from the rest of the computing world. Whichever you use, sooner or later you're going to want access to a spreadsheet, manuscript, database, or graphic that was created on one or the other. Then you'll need to know how to link.

A lot of people use the Apple Macintosh. If the IBM standard has an overwhelming majority, the Mac still has the reputation of being friendly, easy to use, and a great platform for "creative" and graphics applications. Unless you suffer from monomania or actually work for one of the major players, you'll probably agree that it's good that everyone doesn't use the same thing.

If there are fewer reasons to buy a Mac today—IBMs have a pretty fair graphical user interface in Windows, and a top-of-the-line PC will cost less than a comparable Mac Quadra—enough Macs are in use today that it becomes necessary to accommodate them in one way or another.

In addition to the desire to link a PC and a Mac in a desktop environment, linking to a portable is also desirable. People with desktop Macs might want to gather data on the road and use an IBM-standard machine to do so. The PowerBook (the most modern Mac portable) notwithstanding, PC laptops are generally more versatile and less expensive, so if the Mac user can tolerate the PC environment at least part time, this is a good way to go.

Less likely but still possible, a PC person may choose to adopt a PowerBook. In either case, the user needs to have a way to incorporate and transfer remotely gathered files into the desktop environment. More realistically, someone with a PowerBook may drop by to collaborate, and you'll need a way to make the connection.

Traditionally, moving data from one type of computer to another has meant jumping through an aggravating series of hoops. Fortunately, however, hardware and software vendors alike have begun to recognize the importance of making files compatible between PC and Macintosh systems. With a little bit of planning, this once complex job has become manageable, even for the computer neophyte.

Transferring Files Between Macs and PCs

This chapter will describe the ways you can move data from one platform to the other. You will also learn which types of files transfer—and which don't—and a bit about the "tweaking" that is sometimes necessary.

Moving files from platform to platform involves two things: First, you must be sure that the file you want to transfer is formatted in a way that can be read by an application on the other system. Second, you have to physically move the file from one system to another.

Similarly, the link between a PC and a Mac has two steps. The physical link is fairly straightforward, and while it is subject to typical linking anomalies on the PC side (TSRs and the like), once you are connected on the Mac side you'll be ready to go. The hard—or at least harder—part of the PC-Mac bridge has to do with file translation and transfer, so that once a file travels from one place to another, it will be usable in the new format with a minimum of manual reformatting.

REMEMBER: We're talking about moving *data* files. Applications can run only on the computer system for which they were designed. While many software programs are available on both sides of the fence, you can't (for instance) transfer the PC version of Microsoft Word to a Mac and expect it to run.

7

The highest level of file compatibility between platforms is usually provided by companies that have versions of the same program running on both Macs and PCs. The major players in this market are Microsoft with Word and Excel, Lotus with 1-2-3, Aldus with PageMaker, Quark with XPress, and WordPerfect Corporation with WordPerfect. These companies have made sure their files can move from one platform to another while retaining most, if not all, of the vital information. In simplest terms, the Mac and PC versions of these programs speak the same language.

Language, as you may know, includes nuances that may be necessary to get the message across. Translated to computers, this means that a successful link will transfer not only the text, but also its formatting.

What Can You Move?

Usually, word processing files created on a Mac can be used by PC word processors (and vice versa). Many word processing software packages for the Mac can save files in formats that can be used by PC programs. For example, the Macintosh version of Microsoft Word can save files as

Microsoft Word for DOS, and the Windows version can save as Mac files; likewise, WordPerfect for the Mac can save files as PC-compatible WordPerfect files. Documents can also be saved as text or ASCII files, which can be imported into any word processor.

The same concepts apply to spreadsheet data (that usually can be saved in Excel or 1–2–3 format) and graphics (EPS and TIFF are much the same on the Mac as they are on the PC). Other examples of *cross-platform applications* (programs with versions for both the Mac and PC) are Adobe Illustrator, Aldus FreeHand, Excel, Lotus 1-2-3, PageMaker, Ventura Publisher, and Quark XPress.

TIP: If you work in a multiplatform environment and will be translating files between the two, buy software that operates on both platforms. At that point, you are assured that the file created on one will be readable on the other. If not, you can demand that the vendor come to your house and fix it.

The Physical Link

The Mac is made for connectivity, both on a hardware and a software level. As a result, this environment is a lot closer to "plug and play" than the average PC.

The SCSI (Small Computer System Interface) port allows you to connect peripherals, disk drives, tape drives, and the like. Unfortunately, making an SCSI-based PC part of the chain isn't yet possible.

The better news about linking Macs on a physical level is that they are equipped with just two communications ports. There is one less thing to worry about than on a PC—*all* Macs have mouse ports—and the printer and modem ports are identically designed serial connections. This choice is made in software. When you install communications or linking programs, they give you the choice as to which port (modem or printer) to use.

This setup minimizes the need to plug/unplug existing connections, and since printers are often connected through the AppleTalk port, your Mac already has enough ports to make a solid connection.

The best news is that the Mac serial port is a round plug that makes a fast, snug connection. Plugging and unplugging isn't quite the ordeal that it is with PCs.

How Can You Transfer Files?

Regardless of the data you want to move from a Mac to a PC (or a PC to a Mac), you have to decide how you want to accomplish this transfer. There are a number of options—each described in detail later in the chapter.

✦ Transfer files on a network

✦ Use the Mac's SuperDrive

✦ Use the PC's 3 1/2-inch high-density drive

✦ Use an external drive connected either to the Mac or PC

✦ Cable the computers together

✦ Use a modem connection

7

Transferring Files on a Network

A *network* (as you may know) is a series of computers hooked together either to share programs, data files, or resources (like a printer or modem). If your computer is connected to a network that has both Macs and PCs connected to it, you can use the network to move files from one platform to another.

There are different types of networks, and while it is often advertised that all Macs are "network ready," this applies only to LocalTalk or AppleTalk networks, not the kind of networks that can easily mix PCs and Macs.

LocalTalk is Apple's cabling product built into every Macintosh. It allows for a fairly primitive peer-to-peer network for sharing resources like printers or modems. AppleTalk is software built into each Macintosh and into all devices that can network with a Mac. AppleTalk allows file sharing. The networking software is provided by a third party. To connect a PC to an AppleTalk network requires an AppleTalk board and drivers for whatever Mac Local Area Network (LAN) software you are using.

When you connect a PC to an AppleTalk environment it is probably for resource sharing rather than file sharing. For example, connecting through AppleTalk is a commonly used way to give a PC access to an Apple LaserWriter printer.

If you are on a mixed network with PCs and Macs hooked together for file sharing, you are probably using Novell NetWare, Microsoft LAN Manager, or Banyan VINES (with either Ethernet or Token Ring protocols). You may also be in a UNIX environment. Such networks are better choices for platform integration than AppleTalk.

To attach to such a network, the PC needs an interface card and the proper software drivers. The Mac also needs an interface card and software unless the file server includes a LocalTalk card for direct Mac connections.

Once on a network, it's easy to transfer files back and forth between the PC and the Macintosh. If you are on a local area network (LAN) connecting Macintosh and PC computers, convert the Macintosh files into files that can load and then transfer the files directly by using the LAN. Again, this is where it makes the most sense to use software that supports both platforms.

SuperDrive—the Mac's Sneakernet

The Mac has its own version of Sneakernet, where you can exchange files between formats by passing a floppy from one machine to another. A Mac equipped with the 1.44MB SuperDrive has the ability to read 3 1/2-inch DOS disks. If you have read all about the SuperDrive/DOS compatibility, you might be tempted to shove a DOS disk into the Mac drive and expect immediate results. Instead, you'll be notified "This is not a Macintosh disk," and asked "Do you want to initialize it?" You can then either Eject or Initialize. *Don't* initialize! That's the same as reformatting, and all your data will be lost.

Apple File Exchange (AFE)

Before inserting your DOS disk, you must first launch a Mac program called Apple File Exchange (AFE). (This program comes with your System and is usually found in your System folder, where it was placed during system installation.)

After using AFE the first time or two, you'll believe Apple still seems determined to punish users of IBM-standard PCs. AFE's interface and methodology is arcane and primitive—the very antithesis of what you would expect from a Mac. At any rate, once you've launched AFE, you can then insert your DOS disk and have it recognized by the Mac.

AFE gives you several transfer options, DCA-RTF to MacWrite, Text translation, Default, and Other:

✦ *DCA-RTF to MacWrite* Choose this if you are using MacWrite and have saved your DOS files in either DCA or RTF format.

✦ *Text translation* Choose this if you have saved your DOS file as plain ASCII. You'll be given some additional options telling AFE how you want to handle carriage returns (do you want a line feed after each carriage return or not?), special characters (such as control characters and foreign language symbols), tabs (do you want them converted to spaces?), and spaces (do you want them converted to tabs?).

✦ *Default* Choose this if you want to transfer the file without AFE doing any translation. This would be your choice for transferring data from programs like Microsoft Word or WordPerfect—where you are using both a PC version and a Mac version of the software.

✦ *Other* Choose this if you have other translation filters installed. (Apple or other Mac application vendors may include special filters for translation that can be added to AFE.)

7

The Macintosh allows for 31-character filenames with only one illegal character (the colon). The PC allows for eight characters plus a three-character extension. The programs in this section truncate Mac filenames and insert an exclamation point as the first character of the truncated name so that you know it's truncated. You should rename these files using standard DOS filenames.

DOS Mounter

If you plan to regularly use the Mac's SuperDrive to read DOS disks, you should consider DOS Mounter from Dayna Communications—it is much easier to work with than AFE.

DOS Mounter installs as an INIT that makes a DOS disk look like a Mac disk—complete with folders and documents. DOS Mounter can also map the extensions on DOS files. For example, if you transfer a DOS PageMaker file to your Mac, DOS Mounter will also attach a PageMaker icon to the file.

DOS Mounter is compatible with other drives, including DaynaFILE, Bernoulli, SyQuest, Ricoh, and Apple's external 5 1/4-inch drive.

Macintosh PC Exchange

Beginning with System 7.0, Apple began offering extensions to its System software. One of their first products is Macintosh PC Exchange. Working much like DOS Mounter, but with a somewhat more Mac-like interface, Macintosh PC Exchange can mount a DOS disk to open, save, rename, move, copy, or delete PC files.

You can also change the File Creator and Type on files you move from the DOS disk to the Mac, allowing you to launch an application by clicking on the file. Mac files can be moved to the DOS disk for use in the PC.

Access PC

Access PC is similar to the programs just mentioned. It works under System 6 or 7.

Using the PC's Disk Drive

The 3 1/2-inch disk drive you have on your PC can be turned temporarily into a Macintosh-compatible disk drive. There are two ways to accomplish this: PC Deluxe Option Board (hardware) or Mac-in-DOS (software).

PC Deluxe Option Board

If you have a 3 1/2-inch disk drive on your PC, you can use the PC Deluxe Option Board from Central Point Software. The Option Board fits into a slot in your PC and has cables that connect to the floppy drive controller and your disk drive. It gives the drive the ability to read, write, and format Macintosh disks. You can still use your drive as a regular PC drive, in addition to its new capacity to emulate a Mac disk drive. The board works with either a 720K or 1.2MB drive and can read either high- or low-density Mac disks.

Mac-in-DOS

If you have a 1.2MB (high-density) 3 1/2-inch drive in your PC, there is a software program called Mac-in-DOS from Pacific Micro that lets the drive read, write, and format Mac high-density (1.44MB) disks. Mac-In-DOS comes in DOS or Windows versions and is clean and efficient.

External Drives

If your PC doesn't have a 3 1/2-inch drive or if you have an older Mac without the SuperDrive, you can connect an external drive to your computer that can emulate the other platform's floppy disk drive.

PC External Drives

For example, if your PC doesn't have a 3 1/2-inch drive, you can either install one or use an external disk drive like the one from Dayna Communications. The DaynaFILE is an external 3 1/2-inch disk drive that enables your PC to read Macintosh data.

Macintosh External Drives

If your problem is on the Mac side, Apple offers an external floppy disk drive that can read 360K 5 1/4-inch DOS disks. To move files back and forth, you'll need to use AFE or DOS Mounter.

Dayna has both 3 1/2-inch and 5 1/4-inch floppy disk drives called DaynaFILE II that can read regular and high-density PC formatted disks. The 3 1/2-inch drive is SuperDrive compatible and can also read Mac disks, acting like a second disk drive. DaynaFILE II includes a copy of DOS Mounter.

Direct Cable, Modem, and Over-the-Phone Transfers

Another linking method involves the transfer of data via cables. The computers can be directly cabled together or you can use a modem to transfer files over a telephone line.

Hard-Wiring and Telecommunications Software

If both the Macintosh and the PC are in the same room, you can connect them together with a cable and simulate a mode connection by using a communications program (like Crosstalk on the PC and White Knight on the Mac) to transfer the data. If the computers are not in the same room, but each has a modem, you can use the same principle by having one computer call the other one up.

If your sole reason for having the modem and communications software is to transfer files, there are better solutions. This method can be problematic for two reasons: You have to purchase a communications program (either commercial or shareware), and you may need to buy modems, if you don't already have them. You also have to master the communications program for both platforms. Communications can be difficult to comprehend.

File-Transfer Software

Another solution is to use LapLink Mac from Traveling Software or MacLink Plus/PC from Dataviz. Both companies are specialists in moving files from one computer to another. LapLink Mac can move files between PCs and Macs over a modem, over AppleTalk to a Mac, or directly between the serial ports of both the Mac and the PC using an included cable.

Once you've established the connection, you can transfer data from a PC to a Mac at high speeds. Both LapLink Mac III and MacLink Plus/PC have the added advantage that they include the ability to translate between some file formats (for example, WordPerfect to Word) as the files are being transferred. They can also change creator and file type assignments.

If your primary concern is file translation, remember MacLink Plus/PC has more than 400 translation filters and includes a copy of DOS Mounter.

If both the PC and the Mac have modems, LapLink can transfer up to 19,200 baud. With a direct cable connection, the rate is 115,200!

NOTE: With an optional accelerator, Mac-to-Mac transfers can go up to 750,000 baud—handy for moving files back and forth to your PowerBook.

Products like these are popular because they automate most of the communications settings required for transfers.

Using Bulletin Boards to Transfer Files

If you need to transfer files between computers at different locations, a modem might be the answer. An alternative to directly calling the other computer is to use an electronic mail service such as CompuServe Information Service as an intermediary. CompuServe allows your recipient to log on at any time and retrieve the file when it's most convenient.

The drawbacks with modem protocols being intimidating to newcomers still remains. If large files are involved, the fact that transfer rates are limited by the modem's speed may become a factor. If you plan on using modem transfers, using a service like CompuServe may be a good idea for security reasons, since you don't have to leave your computer on and wait for a call all the time with this method, lessening the risk of unauthorized access.

7

 File Translation and Conversion

Moving files from one platform to another is the first step. The second step is ensuring that the guest data can be read by the host program.

This isn't always a problem. For example, PageMaker publications composed on the PC can be transferred back and forth between the Macintosh and the PC without any special translations at all. Everything is intact, including text, formatting, graphics created within

PageMaker, master–page items, bitmapped graphics under 64K, Encapsulated PostScript graphics, and style–sheet information.

But what if you want to transfer a file whose creator doesn't have a counterpart on the other system? In those instances, you will need to find an intermediary format that is supported by both a source and destination systems.

This section discusses both situations.

File and Creator Types

One great feature about the Mac is that each file has an icon (or graphical representation) that matches up with the program that created it. For example, a document created with WordPerfect Mac has an icon that identifies it with the WordPerfect program. If you double-click on the document icon, it launches WordPerfect and automatically loads the document into the program.

How does the Mac know which file goes with which program? It looks at the File Type and Creator Type codes associated with each file. When files are brought from the PC to the Mac, the File and Creator codes are usually not mapped correctly to any Mac application, so the icon is usually generic. If you click on the file icon, you'll get an error message telling you (something like) the application that created the program can't be found.

You can still open the file directly from the application. For example, if the WordPerfect file you brought over from the PC doesn't have a WordPerfect document icon, you can still launch WordPerfect and open the file from the Open dialog box. Once you save the file from within the application, the appropriate File and Creator codes are inserted, and the icon will appear correctly.

Another solution is to use features included in DOS Mounter, LapLink Mac, or MacLink Plus/PC that will insert the correct Creator and File Type codes into your documents as part of the transfer process. MacLink Plus/PC includes a library of more than 400 translation filters that include translations to and from Ami Pro, AppleWorks, MacWrite, Multimate, Officewriter, Professional Write, Wordstar, Works, dBASE, Excel, and Multiplan. It can also handle many graphics conversions.

Text

In the case of word processing documents, most applications can read plain ASCII text files. This solution is best used when you have a simple text file that you haven't spent much time formatting. When a file is saved in ASCII format, almost all formatting is lost. Font specifications, alignment, justification, margins, and tab settings will all have to be reapplied when the document is opened on the new system. If you are a programmer, your best bet is to send files in ASCII format.

If you are using the same word processor like Microsoft Word or WordPerfect on both the PC and the Mac platforms, conversion is simple and reliable. Look in the Save As dialog box and select the format appropriate for the platform you are transferring the document to. (As of this writing, WordPerfect Mac can directly open PC WordPerfect 5.1 and earlier files without any need to do conversion on the PC.)

If you are using different word processors on each platform (for example, Ami Pro on the PC and Word on the Mac) and one program can't directly read the format of another, you'll need to find a satisfactory intermediary format in order to retain your formatting. In other words, you need a format that both programs can reliably read. In the example just given, you could save the Mac Word file in Rich Text Format (RTF), which Ami Pro can read.

While intermediary conversions are a decent workaround, there are potential drawbacks. The major one being the implementation of the export and import filters provided by each vendor. Sometimes the exporting or importing isn't 100 percent reliable, and extraneous characters are introduced, fonts are changed, or the format is altered. Therefore, when using intermediary format or conversion utilities or filters, double-check the final file for formatting accuracy.

Graphics

Both the PC and Mac have a plethora of graphics file formats. You are going to enjoy the best results if you stick with TIFF (Tagged Image File Format) for bitmap or raster graphics and EPS (Encapsulated PostScript) for vector graphics.

Graphics utilities on a PC like Hijaak from Inset Systems are able to convert between a great number of graphics formats. Unfortunately, a similar conversion utility doesn't exist for the Mac. However, MacLink Plus/PC includes many graphics-conversion filters.

Conversion may not be required since most graphics programs can save their files in TIFF or EPS formats. There are several caveats:

✦ There are a number of versions of TIFF, so you may need to convert the TIFF file (using Hijaak on the PC or a shareware Mac utility called FlipTIFF) when moving it from one platform to the other.

✦ EPS files created on one platform may not display a screen image on the other system. This is because the EPS file relies on a bitmap image header for screen-display information. If you save the file in a program like the Windows program CorelDraw, include an image header if you want to later view the file on either the PC or the Mac. Other programs, like Adobe Illustrator or Aldus Freehand, will have Save As options for the other platform.

✦ To print an EPS graphic you must use a PostScript-compatible printer.

If you don't have a PostScript printer, the vector format of choice is PICT2 for the Mac and CGM (Computer Graphics Metafile) or WMF (Windows Metafile) for the PC.

Color Tables   A big issue for anyone who is transferring graphics is color tables. The number of available colors could be different on the sending and receiving machines. To alleviate this problem you can use a nice program called deBabelizer by Equilibrium that allows you to adjust the colors to suit your needs.

Spreadsheets

For spreadsheets, Lotus 1–2–3's WKS or WK1 formats are as close to a universal standard as you're likely to find. This format can be read and written by Excel, Wingz, Quattro, Lotus (of course), and most other spreadsheets. If you are using a program like Excel or Lotus 1-2-3 on both platforms, they will understand their own format from the other platform.

Compressed File Formats

Sometimes, to save space or time during transfer, files or archives are compressed. If you have files compressed on one platform that you want to decompress on another platform, you can usually do this.

In transferring compressed files from the PC to the Mac, the MacBinary option on any file-transfer program should be used. Modem transfers are always in binary, so you needn't worry about this option in such cases.

The most commonly used compression utility for the PC is called PKZip. It creates a file with a ZIP extension. The Macintosh utility Stuffit Deluxe can expand ZIP files.

On the Mac, the compression is usually done either with Compactor or Stuffit. There are several shareware utilities for the PC (Unstuff and Unstuffit) that can decompress Stuffed files.

Transferring Fonts from the Mac to the PC

7

The PC shareware utility, Refont, is capable of moving Adobe Type 1 PostScript fonts from the Mac for use on the PC. Fonts are more like a program than a document. Because of that, you need to be concerned about the internal structure of Macintosh programs, which, unlike PC programs, contain both a data and resource fork. When you move data files, you are only moving data. When you move a font, you must move both the data and the resource.

Considerations in moving a font from the Mac to the PC are as follows:

✦ The font outlines on the Macintosh are the printer fonts. Type 1 fonts reside in the resource fork. So, if you use AFE, the resource information must be copied to the data fork. You can do this in one of two ways. Either use the shareware utility called Refork, or use the program MacBinary. Instructions on how to use each of these is included with the program.

✦ If you use a program like LapLink or MacLink Plus/PC, select the "binary" option when you copy the font from the Mac to the PC. That will preserve the data and resource fork information.

✦ To use a Mac font with Adobe Type Manager (ATM) and Windows, you will need the Type 1 fonts if you plan to use the font's AFM file. (The AFM file is usually included on the disk with the font, but usually *not* copied to the Mac, since few Macintosh programs use the AFM file.)

✦ Once you have moved a copy of the font and its AFM file to the PC, use the shareware utility Refont to create a PFM file from the AFM file and a PFB file from the font. Use ATM to install the font.

TrueType Fonts   TrueType fonts are common on the Macintosh and in Microsoft Windows. You can use a program called Metamorphosis to move TrueType fonts between Windows and the Macintosh. There are shareware programs that accomplish the same task.

Desktop Publishing

The four major DTP programs that are available on both platforms are PageMaker, Ventura Publisher, Framemaker, and Quark Xpress. All of these programs have cross-platform compatibility. PageMaker and Ventura have a few specific requirements that are discussed next.

PageMaker

Aldus claims high levels of compatibility between the PC and Mac versions of PageMaker, and for the most part this is justified. PageMaker transfers are not perfect, however. Some items, such as linked graphic files and vector graphics, must be transferred separately and either placed again in the document or must undergo additional conversion. Other problems can arise if the publication was composed for a type of printer that isn't available to the destination system.

If you've created your document on the PC, you might want higher resolution output than your laser printer is capable of providing. This is where a "service bureau" comes in. Since most service bureaus prefer to do their work on a Macintosh, often files must be moved from your PC to a Mac. This is essential if you are using PageMaker and want any color separations done. Service bureaus often complain of certain problems associated with moving Windows PageMaker files to the Macintosh.

For example, there are differences in font–naming conventions between Windows and the Mac, so you may need to respecify your typefaces.

For example, PageMaker users may find that fonts often have different names on the PC and Mac. PageMaker provides a built-in translation table for some font families, but not all are covered. As a result, when taking a file from the PC to the Mac, some editing may be required to search and rename fonts that have one name on the PC and another on the Mac. If this isn't done, PageMaker merrily prints the page—with the wrong fonts.

Some special characters are mapped differently on the PC than on the Mac. One notable example is with the Zapf Dingbat font trademark and copyright characters. Most foreign characters convert correctly, however. If you use extended characters (over ASCII 126) or Dingbats when taking PC files to service bureaus, you should alert them to any potential problems in advance.

Another potential conflict is that the PC version of hyphenation dictionaries or algorithms may vary slightly from the Mac versions. This could cause the text in documents moved across platforms to reflow differently—changing line endings and page length. The best way to check for this problem is to get a laser proof produced by the system that will be ultimately sending the file to the Linotronics.

Since Aldus regularly updates PageMaker, check in the manual for other system incompatibilities so you will know what changes to make either prior to or after the transfer.

Ventura Publisher

Theoretically, Ventura chapters can be moved between GEM, Windows, and Macintosh environments without losing anything. (Note that Ventura 4.0 and higher files may not be backward compatible with all previous versions of the program; all files from previous versions of Ventura are, however, usable by Ventura 4.0 and higher.)

Ventura Publisher users transferring between platforms may also have font trouble. If the chapter you transfer uses fonts on the PC that aren't available on the Mac (or vice versa), your printer substitutes another in its place. For example, in the case of a PostScript printer, Courier is substituted for unavailable fonts. You must either purchase (or convert) duplicate fonts for the other platform or use another font.

If you have a network, Ventura can access the chapters and their associated files from the server where you have stored them.

PC to Mac   For PC users not on a network, use the Copy All option in the MULTI-CHAPTER dialog box, accessed from the File menu (Windows) or the Options menu (GEM) to copy the files to a disk. You then can give the disks containing the files to the person using the Macintosh version of Ventura.

The Mac user can then access the files using DOS Mounter or AFE. The procedure for doing this is detailed in the Ventura Publisher Macintosh Edition User's Guide that comes with the program.

Mac to PC   To get files from the Mac to your PC involves a different procedure. For text files or graphics, if the Macintosh program can save files in a format that Ventura can load, you can transfer the file from the Mac using one of the following methods:

✦ To directly bring Ventura Mac chapters into Ventura GEM or Windows involves a little extra conversion. If the PC is to access the Mac chapter from a network, all files must be saved in PC format on the central file server. This capability is an option included in Ventura Mac's Copy All function. Using this feature converts all filenames to names the PC can understand. This feature also adds appropriate extensions to the filenames.

✦ Chapters also can be transferred from the Mac to the PC on disks. This transfer is accomplished by using Ventura Mac's Copy All function—copying the files to a DOS disk (using AFE, DOS Mounter, or DaynaFILE).

If the material you transfer uses fonts on one platform that aren't available on another, your printer substitutes another in its place. For example, in the case of a PostScript printer, Courier is substituted for unavailable fonts. You can purchase duplicate fonts for the platform that is missing the font; if the font is on the Mac but not on the PC, you can convert them as described earlier in this chapter.

Running PC Software on a Macintosh

If you have a Mac and need to run a specialized program that only exists on the PC, you can use a program called SoftPC from Insignia Solutions. It's a software-based PC emulator that requires a Mac Plus or later with 4MB of RAM (2MB if you're using System 6). (For the more powerful and faster SoftAT, you need at least a Mac II with 5MB of RAM, 4MB with System 6.)

SoftPC and SoftAT emulate DOS 3.30, but you can upgrade to more recent versions. Regardless of which DOS you use, be forewarned that an emulator is going to run much slower than a dedicated system. You will notice a considerable lag when installing software.

Translations Only

If you only need to translate PC files that have landed on the Mac desktop, DataViz offers a translations-only program. You can use it to convert between hundreds of PC and Macintosh file types to the one you require.

While MacLink Plus/PC includes hundreds of filters for PC programs, translations on the PC can only be done when the PC is linked (via modem or cable) to a Mac.

Software Bridge

7

If you are mainly transferring word processing files, another option is to use Software Bridegroom, from Argosy Software, which can translate between some 30 different word processing formats for both the Mac and the PC. Argosy includes a copy of their MOUNT program, which works like DOS Mounter and Macintosh PC Exchange to allow the Mac to easily mount and access DOS disks.

Preferences

The PC and the Mac are looking more alike. PCs are now graphical, and all "business" application categories have reached maturity on the Mac. Even as the two platforms move toward the middle and do essentially the same thing, there will always be people who prefer one over the other with a passion, and as long as both platforms thrive there will always be a need to link them together—at least once in a while.

We might prefer one or the other, but no one can deny that a two-platform world is a healthy one. This dualism keeps things interesting and moves both parties to greater heights; and as long as there is a way to link diverse computers and exchange information, there can be no losers.

CHAPTER

8

LINKING PCS TO MAINFRAME COMPUTERS

With the rapid changes in computer technology, the demands on the old mainframe-to-workstation model have changed. The same is true of networked PCs. Users want to be able to receive and send e-mail beyond the limits of a local area network. They want to be able to feed and get information from the centralized databases. They want to monitor processes or changes. In order to do this, you have to be able to communicate with the mainframe.

The reasons for you as an independent microcomputer user to want to connect to an IBM mainframe or "host" are growing both in importance and number. Perhaps you want to telecommute to your office from your home PC. Perhaps you are a salesperson who wants to stay in touch with headquarters from the road. Perhaps you need to communicate manufacturing information from the factory floor to the sales office.

Getting Plugged In

This chapter will explain the basics of remote micro-to-mainframe connectivity, and help you understand how all the terminology fits together in a scenario that provides a solution that works best for your situation.

Like they say on TV, "Don't try this at home," meaning, you're going to have to get the help of the people who maintain the mainframe you want to access. They have to have hardware and software in place to accommodate your PC. The challenge of connecting local PCs and LANs to mainframes is answered with a variety of solutions and technologies, which we will not address, but rather will focus on what you, as a remote PC user, need to know to make successful connections.

If you have ever looked at a mainframe screen, you know that mainframe applications don't work the same way PC applications do. Both the structure of the data and user interaction with the machines are different. PCs and PC applications are designed to be intuitive and easy to work with, but you'll probably have to remember obscure commands and procedures to get results from a mainframe. There are some exciting new ways to overcome this difficulty, but let's save that for later.

A whole industry has grown up to solve the problems of connecting microcomputers to IBM mainframes, loosely defined by the term *3270 connectivity*. The 3270 refers to both the protocol and family of display terminals, printers, and control units that were initially designed to interact with the mainframe. When a PC or Macintosh replaces any of these devices, it needs hardware and software that emulate the original device and must use protocols that the mainframe recognizes. In essence, emulation software allows the PC to masquerade as a terminal.

The mainframe sends out all the information about and contained in an application in message units, commonly called 3270 data streams or SNA (IBM's System Network Architecture) data streams to a controller, which in turn interacts with the terminals or PCs. The SNA 3270 data stream itself contains application data, structured field functions, commands, and other control information required by an SNA device. You want as much of this data stream as possible. For example, when you have full access to SNA data streams, you can log on to multiple hosts and use multiple host applications simultaneously, use host graphics, and perform file transfers between the PC and host quickly and reliably using SNA-defined procedures and protocols.

In order to really speak the mainframe's language, your PC has to be able to look and act like the 3270 data terminal the mainframe was designed to interact with. Your screen needs to display the right number of rows and columns—which change from application to application. Your PC needs to support different kinds of keyboards to make sure you can send keystrokes that the mainframe can interpret. You'll want to be able to transfer files efficiently. The software that enables these features also determines what functionality is available. 3270 terminal-emulation software products on the market range from "bare-bones" terminal emulation to sophisticated products that permit automation of traditional command-line/function-key procedures. We'll discuss some of these features later in the chapter.

We're going to focus on what needs to happen on the PC end of the connection and leave the mainframe part of the connection to your MIS department. On the PC end, you have to have some kind of hardware to physically link it to the mainframe—an adapter or modem.

8

Modem Connections

A PC with a modem offers the flexibility to compute at home, in a hotel, at work, or even in an airplane. The challenge is that you still need SNA processing at the workstation to do the things that a mainframe application expects a terminal to do.

There are three major methods of connecting to a mainframe:

✦ *Synchronous Data Link Control (SDLC)*, which uses a special SDLC adapter in the PC and synchronous modems to transmit the native

3270 data stream or an autosynchronous modem plugged into the serial port

✦ *Protocol conversion,* which uses the standard COM port of the PC and Hayes-type asynchronous modems to communicate with a protocol converter that translates between an asynchronous protocol (such as VT100) and the 3270 data stream

✦ *Asynchronous Data Link Control (ADLC),* which also uses the COM port and asynchronous modems, but transmits the actual 3270 data stream

SDLC Modem Links

Synchronous Data Link Control is the IBM standard for connecting remote devices to mainframes. SDLC defines the procedure for establishing, maintaining, and terminating communications between devices in an SNA network. The network could include mainframes, front-end processors, communications controllers, workstations, or printers. SDLC passes native 3270 data streams, which is advantageous because you reliably get all the information about the application.

This method is not without a downside. The primary drawback to SDLC is cost. On the mainframe side, it only plugs into a front-end processor (FEP) that costs a couple of million dollars. Using this resource is also expensive. A port on the FEP can be used for one remote user or for an entire LAN of PCs. Also, the modems required on the PC side are more expensive (and different) than the asynchronous Hayes-type modems many PC users already have. But, if your MIS has made the investment in SDLC, chances are that they will want you to use it.

There are two ways to connect via SDLC. The traditional way is to plug specialized synchronous modems in at both ends for dial-up connection. Unfortunately, these SDLC modems are exclusively specialized, so they cannot enable other communications functions, like accessing ASCII hosts, bulletin boards, electronic mail, and information services. If you're a portable user, you'll have to lug extra hardware in your bag, because the standard asynchronous port or internal modem won't work. If you're a laptop or notebook user, this method may be completely out of the question because you may not have a port available to install an adapter or synchronous modem.

Luckily, now there are autosync modems that can be built into laptops and can serve multiple purposes, although they are still costly.

Protocol Conversion

You may have talked to some people who tell you that they use their Hayes-type modem and dial into their mainframe, no problem. This is true from their standpoint—they use their standard modem to dial a number and they get mainframe data. What they are actually doing, more than likely, is dialing into a *protocol converter*. The protocol converter is typically a small box, residing near the mainframe, that translates between async ASCII terminal-emulation protocols (such as VT100 or VT220) and the 3270 data stream.

While this sounds like a great solution, especially if you have a laptop, there are significant trade-offs. You gain an easily implemented solution. However, you will wait *a lot*. Protocol conversion is very slow. Every time you make a change, the protocol converter will send all the characters for the screen again, instead of just changing the fields you've changed. Also, each character is accompanied with bytes that describe it, called attribute bytes, which also add overhead as they are translated back and forth many times.

8

ADLC Modem Links

There is a little-known way to get connected that allows you to use conventional equipment without sacrificing performance called ADLC (Asynchronous Data Link Control). This approach, originally pioneered by IBM, sends SNA data streams across an asynchronous communications link through a gateway to the workstation. Attachmate's EXTRA! Extended for DOS and EXTRA! for Windows allow you to easily configure an ADLC connection from a remote PC—desktop, laptop, or notebook. No special SDLC adapters or synchronous modems are required, even though full SNA compatibility is preserved at the workstation. Instead of dialing into a protocol converter, a "gateway" system consisting of a PC on the other end of the connection running Attachmate's EXTRA! 3270 Gateway Option reassembles the 3270 information packets as they arrive from the remote PC running EXTRA! workstation software.

The 3270 data stream remains intact between the remote PC and the mainframe, which means that all the automation applications, such as graphical front ends written in Visual Basic, that include HLLAPI calls will still work. HLLAPI provides high-level interface to 3270 control programs for PC applications in BASIC, COBOL, C, or other high-level languages. HLLAPI allows PC programs to communicate directly with the mainframe.

Feature/Function Jigsaw Puzzle

As you may have guessed by now, connecting your PC to a mainframe is not a simple hardware/software installation. You've got to make choices. Once you and your MIS agree on how to connect, you still have to choose software for your workstation. Since interaction with mainframe application presumes that the terminal (PC) will send and receive information in specific predetermined ways, you want to make sure that those capabilities are emulated. If and how these features are implemented will affect your ability to be productive. What follows is an introduction to the core feature set. Then, we'll help you establish a checklist to evaluate the software options.

Keyboard Support

If you look at your PC or Macintosh keyboard, you won't see any keys labeled PF. You would on a genuine 3270 terminal keyboard. Program Function (PF) keys are so central to 3270 communications that they are standard dedicated keys. These functions need to be programmed or "mapped" to keys that are on your PC keyboard.

Unfortunately, there are many versions of keyboards and key layouts, from the old 82-key PC keyboard to the 101-key enhanced versions. You want an easy way to see how to activate the PF keys, commonly a template that is specific to your keyboard. If you want to use the same emulation software in the office and on the road or at home, it will be important that the product support all major keyboards and provide templates to show the location of special keys. Of course, you may want to redefine the function of a specific key—like where the Enter key should be, so you want to make sure that your software makes that reprogramming easy.

Display Ability

3270 terminal displays vary as to screen size, color combinations, and the ability to support specialized features like mainframe graphics, multiple protocols, or multiple sessions. These differences are noted in the four-digit number that describes the display terminal, for example 3178 or 3179-G.

The other significant piece of information is how large (how many rows and columns) the application needs the display to be. This is represented by the terms Model or "Mod" 2, 3, 4, or 5. The reason this is important is that mainframe applications are often written to support a specific type of display device. For example, an accounting package may require a 132-column Model 5 display. Likewise, some applications may require graphics or color. You will want to accommodate all models of terminal display without having to pan or scroll or add special hardware to see oversized screens.

Standard PC screens display 25 lines by 80 columns in text mode (equivalent to Model 2). EGA/VGA displays can add another 18 lines. Clearly, the 80-column limitation can present a problem for the Model 5 132-column display. There are two basic solutions for displaying 132 columns under DOS: use a special graphics adapter that provides more text-mode options in order to display more characters on the screen, or use standard EGA/VGA systems in graphics mode.

With a graphics adapter, the hardware generates the characters. This solution demands custom hardware configuration and is not possible on most laptop systems.

The second alternative for displaying larger screen formats puts EGA/VGA graphics mode to good use. Instead of using the adapter's hardware character generators, the characters are generated in software and displayed as a graphics image on the screen. As graphics images, characters can be reduced in scale without sacrificing the ability to read them.

In Windows, OS/2, and Macintosh operating systems, the display is automatically in graphics mode, which eliminates special text-mode graphics adapters from discussion. Even so, 132 columns of data, along with the window frames and scroll bars, taxes the display space of any monitor. You want to make sure you can easily look at and read all of it.

8

Multiple Sessions

Frequently, when you're interacting with a mainframe, you'll want to be able to have more than one session open at once. That way you can download a file at the same time that you are working in some other application or you can access electronic mail without having to log off that application; you can use two related applications such as order entry and inventory simultaneously.

The number of available concurrent sessions varies between 3270 products. Actually, you'll probably never use more than two or three concurrently. More is not necessarily better, particularly if the product runs on DOS-based PCs and allocates memory buffers for sessions not in use.

File Transfer

One of the most common uses of the micro-mainframe connection is to transfer files. All major emulation-software vendors offer file-transfer support, although the performance can vary dramatically. You need to work with your MIS to find out which of the major methods you should use—IND$FILE, Structured Fields, or OV/MVS.

If you run your e-mail system using Office Vision/MVS, formally known as PS/CICS, also called OV/MVS, support for it in your emulation software is important. Otherwise, you'll use IND$FILE "buffered" or "structured" fields.

Here's how file transfer works. File transfer starts at the PC with a command at the DOS prompt, such as the following command line:

    receive test txt b:test.txt (ascii crlf

This command executes the IND$FILE program on the mainframe and requests that the "test txt" file be sent by the mainframe to the "B" window in the PC. Because the command specifies an ASCII file, the mainframe must translate the data from EBCDIC (the mainframe language) to ASCII, which is used by the PC. There are two methods for transferring the files between the PC and the mainframe: buffered file transfer and structured fields file transfer.

The Buffered Method

With the buffered method, the mainframe, before sending data, converts the binary value into a sequence of two printable characters. The first character selects one of four conversion tables. The second character selects the converted byte in the specified table. (The second character can never be the same as one of the four first character possibilities.)

As each byte is converted, the mainframe determines whether it needs to select one of the other tables. If it does not need to select another table, the first byte is not sent, since only the second byte is necessary for conversion.

When a new table is needed the first character will again precede the second character. The new table selection will be in effect until another first character is sent. This method allows the 256 possible binary combinations of each byte to be sent over the mainframe-PC communications link as a character that will not interfere with control codes.

Structured Fields

The second method of transfer uses structured fields to send blocks of binary information directly from the mainframe to the PC. This method still requires that the mainframe translate EBCDIC to ASCII if the ASCII option is specified, but the error checking and translation is done on blocks rather than individual characters. The size of these blocks, commonly referred to as the *data buffer size*, can vary from 2K to 32K bytes. The fewer blocks, the fewer translations and error checks. So, the larger you can make your blocks, the better overall transfer rate you'll get. However, you must be prepared to pay for this increased performance with more memory at the workstation. A 32K buffer, for example, requires 32K of memory.

With this basic understanding, you can appreciate what needs to be done to make the characters appear correctly on your PC. The language translation problem stems from the fact that the translation occurs inside an IND$FILE when translating to and from EBCDIC and ASCII.

8

Background Send/Receive

On DOS-based PCs, IND$FILE usually runs as a DOS application, which means that you can either transfer a file or work in a PC program. Some 3270 software products offer IND$FILE as a background task, so you can have the machine work for you while you work, as well. While this isn't an issue in Windows, OS/2, and Macintosh operating systems, if you are operating in DOS, you will want to make sure that you can run PC programs in the foreground while file transfer takes place.

Variable Buffer Sizes

You can improve performance with variable data buffer sizes. The data buffer size is the size of the block of bytes (from approximately 2000 up to about 32,000) being transferred. If you increase the data buffer size, you decrease the number of acknowledgments, needed after each block is received, between the two computers. This results in faster performance. As usual, increased speed comes with a price, in this case more memory at the workstation. Depending on your circumstances you will want a product that offers variable buffer sizes, so you can balance speed against memory.

Printer Emulation

If you are in a remote location and you want to print out some of this information you're getting, you're going to need to have a printer that the mainframe can address. With DOS, you'll need to check to see if the specific printer driver is included in the 3270 software. Windows, OS/2, and Macintosh provide support for many printers within the operating system.

An alternative to printer emulation is the "print to disk" feature. If you can route the mainframe print job to your hard disk, you can print the file at your convenience. The mainframe's managers will like this solution because it minimizes the time you're connected to the mainframe. You'll get several advantages as well: it's fast, and it comes to you in the form of a report, with recognizable columns and rows.

Memory Consumption

With advanced operating environments like Windows, OS/2, and the Macintosh, memory consumption is less of an issue than it is with DOS. However, you always want to make sure that you have enough memory to run your PC application. The ability to address extended memory removes the traditional 640K limitation of DOS and places less pressure to conserve every byte.

If you are still using DOS, products like DOS 5 (and thereafter), DESQview, or Software Carousel can ease the memory crunch, but you can't just swap out the 3270 software like other PC applications. The 3270 software must maintain constant communications with the mainframe. You need to make sure that the software is designed to be able to free up the memory it doesn't need, at the same time as it protects the persistence of functions that you do need—the communications link, file transfer, and printer emulation—if you decide to suddenly swap to a different application.

The Good News: You Can Automate!

8

If you remember the old days of PC programs, when you were greeted by a blinking "dot" prompt and expected to remember what to do on your own, you know how far PC programs have come. Now, emulation software is doing the same thing for the mainframe screen. The advantages of an automated approach are immediately obvious when you look at a mainframe screen versus a graphical representation of the data.

Doing routine tasks like logging on to the host and transferring a file that you work with regularly can be time consuming and tedious. Likewise, transferring information from a mainframe application into your PC program can mean manually reentering the keystrokes, but some 3270 terminal-emulation software enables you to simplify and automate these processes.

For example, many 3270 emulators on the market offer macro-recording capability. Some offer a scripting language for programming more complicated routines. You can use these macro-recording and scripting capabilities to build routines for accessing the mainframe, transferring files, and other routine tasks. You also may be able to create routines to exchange information between the terminal emulator and other applications running on the PC.

When the 3270 emulator includes "Application Programming Interfaces" (APIs) such as HLLAPI and DDE, you can use programming tools like Toolbook, Visual Basic, C, Pascal, and others to create customized user interfaces that replace the terminal-emulation screen.

Why Is It Worth All the Trouble?

Connecting to the mainframe may be complex, but you can reap both tangible and intangible benefits. Skipping the morning commute or enjoying more time at home are certainly inviting reasons to be able to work from a home computer. Some are using this ability as a way to be able to change their lives. If you can get at all the information you need to do your job, supply all the information expected of you to others, and stay in touch with all the people involved in your projects, then choosing your workplace becomes an option.

This kind of connectivity is not just for personal convenience. Here are a few real-life examples of how single PCs connected to mainframes can affect business.

✦ At a company in the midwest, salespeople carry laptops out to customer sites. They place customer orders directly into the company's central order/entry program, which in turn checks on inventory and arranges shipping. All this is done without having to write up or process any paper forms. The salesperson can tell the customer immediately when the product will be available and how much it will cost.

✦ A manufacturer is able to monitor real-time processes from a laptop on the factory floor. They are able to closely monitor production so they can accurately predict the amount of raw materials in stock to meet current and coming demands.

◆ A state department of highways has equipped a van with a video camera and PC and sent it out to record every foot of road in the state. The accumulated information will be stored in the state's mainframe and analyzed for making maintenance plans for the next several years.

◆ Police departments are adopting the technology in droves, well, driving. They are outfitting their squad cars with computers that connect to the county databases via radio modems. These links are providing them with more information, more quickly, when they want to know about a car or driver they have pulled over.

Summary

PC-to-mainframe communication is complex. Here's a checklist to help you evaluate key areas needed in terminal-emulation software.

Keyboard Support

◆ Are all major PC and Macintosh keyboards supported?

◆ Is user remapping supported?

◆ Does the product include layout templates to easily locate special 3270 function keys?

8

Display Ability

◆ Does the product support Models 3, 4, and 5?

◆ When the characters are reduced in size, are they still easy to read?

Multiple Sessions and PC-DOS Concurrency

◆ Does the product support multiple mainframe sessions?

◆ Does the product only allocate memory to selected sessions?

◆ Is PC DOS concurrency available?

◆ Can you turn it off while the program is active?

File Transfer

✦ Does IND$FILE utilize structured fields?

✦ Does IND$FILE support variable data buffer sizes?

✦ Will IND$FILE operate as a background task in DOS?

✦ Will Import/Export operate as a background task in DOS?

Printer Emulation

✦ Is printer emulation available?

✦ Is "print to disk" supported?

✦ Are both serial and parallel ports supported?

Memory Consumption

✦ For a given set of features, how much memory does the product require?

✦ Is there sufficient memory left over to run PC applications?

✦ Does the product support the DOS 5 (and above) task swapper and third-party memory-management tools?

✦ Will functions like printer emulation and file transfer continue to run if the 3270 software is swapped out of main memory?

Automation Considerations

✦ Does the product support a macro recorder and editor?

✦ Will the same automation routines and customized user applications run across any connection (LAN, SDLC, ADLC) without modification?

✦ Are special utilities available to streamline applications development using tools like Visual Basic?

HLLAPI

✦ Does the product support HLLAPI?

✦ If it's a Windows product, does the HLLAPI implementation provide task switching so that more than one application can communicate with the mainframe simultaneously?

DDE

✦ If it's a Windows product, does it support Dynamic Data Exchange (DDE) and Dynamic Link Libraries (DLLs)?

✦ Does the DDE support include extended functionality that allows full host control from another PC application such as Word for Windows or Excel?

8

CHAPTER

Hot Links

WIRELESS LINKS

Cabling has always been more trouble than it's worth. The stuff is messy, expensive, and difficult to install without disrupting ongoing business. Moving a network device across the room might take five minutes, but running new wire to the new location can take half a day, with installers sprinkling ceiling tile crumbs on workers below them. The constant restructuring characteristic of corporate life in the '90s means that people and their computers move around a lot more often; recabling costs have skyrocketed.

Wireless connections are becoming more important as computers and their users become more mobile. Corporate strategies such as cutting response times and increasing worker productivity often hinge on putting people and computers where no wire has gone before. Empowerment strategies might require making all pertinent information and computing resources available to every employee all the time, even if that means putting a link in an airplane or commuter train.

Wireless generally means radio frequency (RF) or infrared light radiation modulated to carry digital signals. The process is fundamentally the same as wired data transmission, but the exposure of digital signals to "open air" hazards creates a unique array of problems, solutions, and limitations for wireless links.

Infrared Light Links

Hewlett-Packard's 95LX palmtop computer provides a technically simple example of wireless linking's potential. Infrared light allows two 95LXs to exchange files at distances up to eight inches. Motorola has a wireless pager that plugs into a 95LX, allowing users to receive text and numbers from a central computer while they're in the field. 95LX owners can download their latest spreadsheets and share them at meetings, update data while in those meetings, even retrieve and get to work on last night's numbers while the commuter train rolls along.

Printer sharing is another application for wireless links. Infrared light can be used when linking is needed in a single room. Infralink of America, Inc., (Arlington, VA) makes an IR system that can connect up to eight PC users to a single printer, at distances up to 230 feet. Infralink units plug into the parallel ports of PCs and printer and achieve speeds of up to 237 Kbps.

The Infralink beam is diffused to make line-of-sight alignment of sending and receiving units less critical. The company refers to this diffused beam as "broadcast infrared," and claims no special alignment is needed for distances up to 23 feet. Diffused IR is handy in a room where devices are frequently moved (such as a warehouse full of workers with hand-held terminals) or where cubicle walls and irregular ceiling features may obstruct the IR light. However, signal strength declines more rapidly with distance than it does in a tighter beam.

Photonics Corp., the pioneer in infrared networking, provides an AppleTalk/LocalTalk IR transceiver called PhotoLink. The transceivers (one per network node) are all aimed at a common point on the ceiling, where they bounce their beams of light to one another. (A green light on each unit lets you know when it is properly aligned and receiving signals.) Photolink units operate at 230 Kbps for up to 200 meters (a pretty big room!).

True LAN connections allowing interactive use of remote software demand speeds in excess of 2 Mbps. InfraLAN, from BICC Data Networks, more than meets the challenge with a Token-Ring system running at speeds up to 100 Mbps. The Travelers Corp. has tested a 20-user InfraLAN with excellent results for over a year. Travelers' Nick Balensky says the company turned to infrared because offices were being rearranged more often and recabling costs became excessive. Balensky says the InfraLAN has been totally transparent to users, fully Token-Ring compatible, and much faster and simpler to install.

Infrared light has some unique benefits, including security from eavesdropping, immunity to interference from radio frequency sources, and freedom from FCC regulation, but light cannot tolerate physical obstruction at all; room-to-room connections are impractical. Even a 20-foot window-to-window link between buildings is too much for infrared during snow or heavy rain. (Such an arrangement might work in sunny Arizona—until the window-washers' scaffold drops by.)

9

Radio Links

Radio frequency links are more forgiving. In fact, for distances up to 20 miles, RF can be the most cost-effective way to link buildings and remote user groups. RF supports more applications than infrared—and comes with a broader range of potential problems.

One of the most important issues when considering RF linking is whether you need an FCC-licensed technology. The airwaves are getting crowded; you might not be able to get permission to use the necessary frequencies in a metropolitan area. That still leaves unlicensed options such as spread-spectrum RF.

Since 1985, the FCC has allowed unlicensed operation of devices using up to one watt of power in three frequency bands, called ISM bands. To minimize interference, FCC regulations require ISM devices to use *spread-spectrum transmission* technology. Briefly, spread-spectrum distributes the signal's energy over several frequencies in the ISM range, resulting in lower signal strength on any given frequency and less opportunity for interference. The receiving station retrieves the signal from the various frequencies according to a predetermined protocol.

All this encoding and decoding slows down spread-spectrum links. NCR's WaveLAN achieves 2 Mbps throughput at up to 100 meters, the fastest spread-spectrum LAN available and barely adequate for running remote software. O'Neill Communications' LAWN (Local Area Wireless Network) is even slower at 19.6 Kbps, but comparable to most peer-to-peer networks and adequate for electronic mail, printer sharing, and small file transfers. LAWN is particularly useful in home-office situations. It performs well through residential walls and floors, and its FCC Class B certification means it won't interfere with other computing devices, VCRs, garage door openers, and so on.

Licensed RF: Greater Speeds and Ranges

A licensed frequency eliminates the need to use spread-spectrum and improves network speed, at the cost of more limited range thanks to FCC-mandated power restrictions. Motorola Radio/Telephone Systems Group's Altair system provides wireless in-building Ethernet compatibility at 10 Mbps. Up to 32 User Modules can share a single central Control Module, and each UM can support up to four daisy-chained workstations. The 25-milliwatt power restriction limits UM-to-CM range to 130 feet in open air or about 40 feet through three interior (hollow) walls. Floors and load-bearing walls will kill Altair's signal.

Altair provides transmission security between UM and CM in two ways. Each UM sends its Ethernet address when it signals the CM, and the CM responds with an encryption key used in subsequent transmissions. The network administrator can also give the CM a list of up to 32 UMs authorized to access the network; any other UM attempting to log on will be ignored.

Boeing Computer Services, Inc., has run tests on a 20-user Altair system and says users notice no performance difference between air and wire. Tests conducted by Howard Eglowstein at *BYTE* magazine found no speed difference when transferring files on a UNIX LAN using TCP/IP.

But he ran into serious performance degradation when running Novell Netware. Larges files copied at 194 Kbps across wire, but slowed to 69 Kbps or less on Altair. Eglowstein notes, "When NetWare operates, each transmitted packet requires a response. . .Altair's radio protocol adds to each packet a bit of overhead that can slow down the network considerably" (*BYTE*, July 1991). Application software run across the Altair network was also "noticeably slowed but acceptable."

More users are jumping into the RF game, creating a political battle for licensed airwave space the likes of which has not been seen since the Bell companies were forced to open their networks to customer-owned equipment and alternative carriers. Apple has petitioned the FCC to designate 40MHz in the 1.8 to 2GHz microwave band exclusively for data communications. The FCC's own engineering studies have found that this band is about the only feasible space available for the new generation of wireless communications. However, the bandwidth is currently allocated to a variety of energy utilities and agricultural users, who are vociferously upset about the idea. Apple and other proponents argue that the bandwidth is grossly underutilized, and the FCC has basically told the current tenants, "use it or lose it."

Mobile Links for Laptop Road Warriors

9

While microwave systems are certainly moveable, they are not all that mobile. Broadcast systems like Altair are deliberately limited in range, while long-haul microwave links (up to 20 miles) are tightly focused beams; users cannot move around much at either end. The truly footloose and fancy-free computerist needs the ability to send and receive data from anywhere over any distance.

Currently, two mobile data options are available: cellular phone and public radio networks. Cellular has the advantages of ubiquity and market competition; any cellular operator will be glad to carry your data as well as voice transmissions. Public radio packet-switched networks are designed exclusively for data transmission. Their packetized architecture protects data from many of the perils of over-the-air transmission discussed in the following sections. Unfortunately, packet-net services are only available in a relatively limited number of major markets and are dominated by two major players.

Both methods offer the mobility users need. Neither is any kind of speed demon; typical file-transfer rates are in the 4.8 to 19.2 Kbps range. But users' applications rarely involve large file transfers. Data collection, time-sensitive e-mail, and short database inquiries all benefit from mobile data networks.

The benefits have to add up fast, because the cost of mobility does. Radio modems can cost $1,700, while integrated laptop/phone rigs climb into the $5,000 to $7,000 range. Even a simple hand-held radio terminal can cost $2,000. After buying the hardware, expect to pay dearly for air time. Typical public radio users spend $70 to $120 per month. Cellular charges are 60 to 85 cents per minute.

Cost Savings and a Competitive Edge

Many companies *do* find favorable cost/benefit ratios in going wireless. Federal Express built its own radio network starting in 1977 at a cost of several hundred million dollars, but the competitive advantage of being able to instantly trace any package anywhere, any time, more than outweighed the huge investment. Compared to FedEx's expenditures, today's service options look cheap and can be highly profitable in productivity.

Maersk, Inc., a Danish shipping company, reduces delivery delays due to lost containers by employing hand-held radio terminals to instantly record inventory in a central database. Co-Op Building Consultants used to take ten days to assess fire or hurricane damage and get claims paperwork to insurance companies. Today its field adjustors, armed with laptops and cellular phones, do the job in 90 minutes. President Clay Page says, "We can handle about 60 percent more work with the same number of people."

Cellular Phone Modems: Affordable, Useful, and Precarious

Even small consultants can benefit from occasional use of mobile data links. Anita Wilburn Dorsett, President and CEO of Executive Information Service, puts her cellular-linked laptop to use when demonstrating her firm's online search capabilities to prospective clients. Dorsett says, "When they see what online searching can accomplish, then they understand what we take for granted." She adds that a cellular modem is preferable to asking the client for use of his phone lines, which may be considered an imposition and often is impossible anyway. PBX switchboards often can't be used by modems, and meeting rooms generally don't include phone jacks.

ARDIS, a joint venture of IBM and Motorola, and RAM Mobile Data provide most of the packet-switched long-haul service in the U. S. The FCC licenses the bandwidth to the companies, which in turn charge customers a monthly fee for use of specific frequencies in certain areas. Both vendors sell or lease mobile data communications equipment too. ARDIS, in fact, tends to dictate what equipment customers will use by making its services highly reliant on Motorola equipment. IBM's PCRadio will operate only on ARDIS or other Motorola-based public networks.

Cellular data communication allows greater choice of equipment, as long as certain basic requirements are met. Chief among these is an RJ-11 interface, which provides a standard modular phone jack for connecting the modem to the cellular phone, and a simulated dial tone, without which the modem will never know it's connected. RJ-11 interfaces come in a bewildering variety. Some are designed to work with only one vendor's cellular phones, others support just a few phones. Some cellular modems come with built-in RJ-11s, another item to check before you rush out and buy a separate unit.

Error-correction protocols are virtually essential for cellular data links. Every cellular phone user has experienced fading, line static, "handoff" interruptions moving between cells, and "dead spots" from which cellular just can't make a connection. These things are inconvenient for voice communication but often deadly when transmitting data.

9

Error correction can be performed in a cellular modem's hardware or in the user's terminal software (like ProComm or Crosstalk), but the same error-correction protocol must be in effect at both ends of the connection. Naturally, things are complicated by a variety of competing error-correction "standards." Spectrum Cellular effectively promotes its SPCL protocol, installed in many existing cellular services. Microcom has introduced its own line of cellular modems equipped with MNP Class 10 error correction, and has licensed MNP-10 to Rockwell as well. Telebit's PEP protocol is a minor but noteworthy third runner in the protocol race.

Cellular modem manufacturers will eventually give up trying to capture the standard trophy, as they did in the mainstream modem market. We should see cellular modems supporting both MNP-10 and SPCL, as most high-speed modems sold today support both MNP-5 and v.32. Meanwhile, if you must buy a one-protocol cellular modem, consider buying SPCL and using terminal software that supports MNP-10. Then you can switch from hardware-based to software-based error-correction when necessary. MTEZ software from MagicSoft offers an MNP-10 add-in module touted for cellular communicators.

Handoff interruptions occur when a cellular phone user moves from one cell to another and can last up to 1.2 seconds. Most modems disconnect after waiting 0.5 seconds for a lost carrier to be restored. The simple solution with Hayes-compatible modems is to issue the command **ATS10=12** to force the modem to wait up to 1200 milliseconds for the carrier to return before disconnecting.

Given all the potential gotchas involved when mating cellular phone, RJ-11 interface, computer, and terminal software, it makes sense to buy as much equipment as possible from a single vendor in an integrated package. Buyers who lack both laptop and cellular phone can get the whole works in one suitcase from ITC, Spectrum Cellular, NEC, or Toshiba. Laptop owners can buy cellular phone, modem, and RJ-11 interface in one package from Spectrum Cellular, Eagle Cross, and Vital Access. Cellular modems with integrated RJ-11 and error-correction can be had from Microcom, Spectrum Cellular, or Toshiba America. Motorola makes an RJ-11 interface, but, typically, supports only its own cellular phones. Telular, Inc., makes a more versatile interface device.

The Near (?) Future of Cellular Data Networks

Current cellular phone technology is expensive and unreliable compared to the wired network. Some metropolitan markets, such as Los Angeles, have become saturated with cellular phone users; it can be hard enough to find a clear channel on which to call a tow truck, let alone CompuServe. The quality of cellular connections has never been satisfactory for voice, and data transfers are more seriously affected by line noise. Mobile phone battery life is shorter than a mayfly's.

Two solutions to this litany of woe are on the drawing boards. Don't look for either to appear before 1994, or to be in usefully widespread operation before 1995, but keep your eyes peeled for announcements of their introduction.

Personal Communication Networks (PCNs)

Ameritech and other phone companies are field-testing a new generation of low-powered, very compact cellular systems designed to provide voice and data links of hardwired quality. The low power of these systems will permit phones and modems to shrink to the size of a deck of playing cards; base stations will become desktop rather than room-sized machines. Lower power also means longer battery life.

The range of each cell will also shrink, to as little as a few hundred feet. Smaller cells mean fewer users competing for channels in any given cell, so L. A. and other overcrowded markets will again be able to add users. Smaller cells also imply more cells to cover a given region, so handoffs from one cell to another will happen more often as users toodle along the road. Unless the new technology does a better job of minimizing the momentary loss of carrier during handoff, data transmissions might be even more precarious than they are now.

Cellular Digital Packet Data (CDPD)

9

IBM Corp. and the nine largest cellular carriers in the U. S. are developing Cellular Digital Packet Data (CDPD) to carry digital data over the existing cellular phone system. CDPD relies on the fact that there is always a good deal of "dead air" in a voice conversation—snippets of time in which a cellular channel is not used by the callers at each end. By breaking data transmissions into short packets and broadcasting them during these gaps in voice traffic, CDPD should be able to accommodate substantial increases in data traffic without competing with voice callers for cellular channels. The cellular carriers love this idea, since they will not have to replace or add to all their existing equipment. Many of the new developments use the newest form of computer miniaturization, "little tiny computers," which will be discussed in Chapter 10.

End users: hold on to your wallets—many PCNs and CDPD products will require new species of modems, phones, and other equipment.

CHAPTER

Hot Links

NEW LINKING CHALLENGES: LITTLE TINY COMPUTERS

Palmtops, pentops, and personal digital assistants are all small hand-sized computers, about the same size as a thick checkbook. They weigh in at a pound or less and run on AA batteries. This diminuitive size has led some people to call them LTCs—Little Tiny Computers.

LTCs have largely been used as computerized day books. Most palmtops sold these days are designed to be business units. They combine programs in ROM for storing and recalling telephone numbers and addresses, business card information, memos, appointments, and schedules. Many LTCs also tell you the time in any of several time zones you specify and ring alarms; and, of course, you can use an LTC as a calculator.

A Brief History of LTCs

There have been a number of hand-held computers in the last decade, including the HP 75, the Sharp 1200, and the Casio FX-702P. All of these were relatively small and lightweight by the standards of the time. They did not have a lot of memory or processing power, and the batteries were either too heavy for really portable operation or too weak for long periods of cordless operation. None of them were particularly successful.

The most popular of the first LTCs were the Casio B.O.S.S. and the Sharp Wizard. These tended to have very small screens and chiclet keyboards. While the B.O.S.S.'s keyboard had a QWERTY arrangement, the Wizard's had an ABC structure. Each had proprietary processors and ROM cards. With limited connectivity options, these were used primarily as stand-alone units for taking notes and entering addresses and numbers.

Following the B.O.S.S. and the Wizard were contemporary units like the Poqet PC and the HP 95LX. These were built with an eye toward DOS compatibility and file exchange. Serial links were added as well as expansion options, centered on the PCMCIA (Personal Computer Memory Card Industry Association) standard. The keyboards stayed about the same, but the screens got bigger—8 lines of 40 characters—and easier to read.

Although Canon's AI Note was the first pen-based computer on the market, Sony's PTC-500 was the first pen-based computer to sell well. The PTC-500 is actually a "subnotebook" rather than a pentop: larger than a palmtop but thinner and lighter than a notebook computer. Sony has since introduced pentop models, the PTC-300 and the PTC-310, which are sold only in Japan at this time.

Most LTCs these days are built around the Personal Computer Memory Card Industry Association (PCMCIA) standard, developed by a number of hardware and software companies. The PCMCIA standard lets LTCs use modems, networking cards, and *flash cards*, solid-state memory devices that use static RAM, which does not need refreshing and thus reduces the load on the battery. The recent 2.0 version of the PCMCIA standard addresses radio communications, mass storage devices, and I/O capability for LANs and other peripheral functions.

Palmtops

The typical *palmtop* computer uses a "clamshell" design with two hinged halves. Keyboards use chiclet-style keys. The current crop of palmtops tend to have 40-character, 8- or 16-line liquid crystal screens. Many LTCs also have a touchpad for accessing programs in ROM.

Newer palmtops are almost as powerful as some of the less expensive notebook computers, and have a couple of other advantages besides: palmtops cost a fraction of the price of notebooks and last as much as 20 times longer on a single battery charge—and palmtops weigh almost nothing. For example, when the Florida Department of Transportation tried to do a survey using seven-pound notebooks, they rapidly discovered the notebooks were too heavy. When surveyors shifted to HP 95LXs, they simply clipped the palmtops to their clipboards.

Many companies are producing memory expansion devices for LTCs. Stac Electronics (known for Stacker, its popular disk-compression utility) and ACE Technologies (makers of memory and storage devices for palmtops and portable computers) have created the DoubleCard, a plug-in card that doubles the amount of space on a standard palmtop RAM card. The DoubleCard works with many palmtops, including the Poqet, the HP 95LX, and other DOS-compatible units that use the PCMCIA interface.

10

The HP 95LX

The $799 HP 95LX, shown in Figure 10-1, is the first palmtop to feature Lotus 1-2-3 built into ROM. The HP 95LX runs DOS 3.2, Lotus 1-2-3 version 2.2, and half a dozen different applications on a DOS machine using 1 megabyte of memory. There are hundreds of applications now that work with the HP 95LX.

The screen is 16 lines by 40 characters, which means that software must be tailored to fit the HP 95LX's display requirements. Lotus, for example, displays some of their longer menus in two lines.

The HP 95LX
Figure 10-1.

Hewlett-Packard has released a separate 1-megabyte memory card for the HP 95LX, which lets you run larger spreadsheets with the built-in version of Lotus 1-2-3. Because the HP 95LX conforms to the PCMCIA standard, Poqet Computer RAM cards and Intel Flash cards will also work. You can buy Flash cards with up to 4MB. Many third-party applications that have been cramped by the memory limits on the HP 95LX can run or run better with the additional room.

Macintosh users will be interested to know that MacLink Plus for the HP 95LX from DataViz lets you back up, transfer, and translate files between a Macintosh and the HP 95LX. Meeting Maker from On Technology lets you organize and schedule meetings using the HP 95LX and a Macintosh. Notify! from Ex Machina lets the HP 95LX receive information from Macintosh mail systems and network management programs. There is also a Macintosh connectivity kit from Sparcom for general information transfers between the HP 95LX and a Macintosh.

Skystream is a three-ounce satellite paging receiver that receives text from Skytel Corp.'s satellite network. The $399 Skystream module connects to the HP 95LX's serial port. It can store up to 32K of data for later downloading to the HP 95LX even when it is not attached.

Serial links are not the only means of exchanging information. Some of the newer LTCs use IR links. These IR links let you exchange data by aiming two like LTCs at each other and establishing a link. You can use the IR (infrared) links to synchronize files and exchange selected information. For example, ACT! is software for the HP 95LX. It lets you exchange information through the HP 95LX's IR connections. Just line them up and press Ctrl-Z to "zap" information between the two. You can transfer business cards, phone numbers, addresses, or any other information stored on the HP 95LX.

Besides LTC-to-LTC connections, you can also connect an LTC to another device using the IR interface. Extended Systems in Boise, ID, has created the JetEye printer module, a $129 IR module that receives information from the HP 95LX's IR interface. The JetEye plugs into the parallel port of an HP LaserJet printer and a standard Centronics cable, but does not interrupt the normal flow of data to the printer.

The Psion Series 3

The $495 Psion Series 3 uses a NEC V30H (8086-compatible) chip and comes with 256K of RAM. Two solid state disk (SSD) drives can store 4 megabytes of information online. You can also store data in DOS-compatible files on removable Flash cards.

The Series 3 uses a proprietary operating system with attractive pull-down menus. The operating system supports task switching, so you can move between applications while they're running. Advanced users can use Psion's OPL/w, a proprietary programming language similar to BASIC and Pascal, to write procedures that pass values to the calculator. In addition to the standard LTC applications, the Series 3 comes with a sophisticated WYSIWYG word processor capable of reading Microsoft Word files. Text attributes such as bold and italics appear on the screen.

You can connect the Psion Series 3 to PCs, Macintoshes, printers, and modems through an optional serial link and a communications package with scripting features.

10

Pentops

One of the major complaints about palmtop computers is that in order to make a really convenient pocket computer, you have to sacrifice the room for a usable keyboard. Most palmtops have small, chiclet-style keys set very close together. Even with the keys laid out in the standard QWERTY layout, most users are not able to type effectively on a palmtop.

Enter *pentops*. Pentops are palmtops that use a pen interface rather than a keyboard. You write on a digitizing screen using a stylus or "pen." Pens are used in two ways. Most commonly, the pen can act like a "supermouse," pointing to items and menu options, dragging items from one place to another, drawing lines, and so on. Like other graphically oriented interfaces, pen-based systems are generally more intuitive.

Some pentops are also able to recognize handwritten input. You write something on the screen, and the computer looks at your input, matches it to characters, and processes it accordingly. Remember how your second-grade teacher chided you about your messy printing? Neatness does count here. Pentops can decipher a wide range of handwriting styles, although they can't handle cursive yet. At this time, there are not a lot of pentops that can do handwriting recognition.

Hewlett-Packard is not releasing a pentop version of its popular HP 95LX until Intel 80386 chips are available for palmtop computers. According to HP product manager Marcia Coffey, "You really need [a 386 chip] to do handwriting recognition properly."

The two best known pen interfaces are Microsoft's PenWindows and GO's PenPoint. PenWindows is a version of Windows that uses pen input. Because PenWindows is based on Windows, it can run current Windows applications. At this time, there are no LTCs running PenWindows, but increasing power and storage capacity in many upcoming units may make this a possibility in the next year or so. GO's PenPoint is being used for a number of new personal digital assistants, which are discussed in the next section.

Sharp Wizard OZ-9600

Listing at about $700, the Sharp Wizard OZ-9600, shown in Figure 10-2, is a hybrid unit: it has a keyboard and a mouse-like pen interface. You use the keyboard as the primary source of input. The pen is used for selecting icons or fields on the screen. You can also draw or write with

The Sharp
Wizard
OZ-9600
Figure 10-2.

the pen, but the information is saved as graphics. The Sharp Wizard
OZ-9600 doesn't do handwriting recognition.

The Sharp Wizard OZ-9600 does not follow any of the existing
standards for LTCs. The operating system is proprietary, it doesn't have
a PCMCIA port, and the serial port is not an RS-232. Although you can
plug the unit into your PC, you can't use any of your existing modems,
fax/modems, or other serial devices. Sharp's 1200-baud Wizard modem
costs $179, and their send-only fax/300-baud modem is $499, both of
which are extremely pricey in today's market. All the Sharp Wizard
cards for earlier versions of the Sharp Wizard will be compatible with
the OZ-9600, but you won't be able to use any of the PCMCIA cards.

The Sharp Wizard OZ-9600 comes with an IR interface. You can transfer
information between two Wizard OZ-9600s by lining up the IR links
(like you can with the HP 95LX and other LTCs). You can also buy an
IR link that plugs into your desktop computer or a printer. This link,
though not yet released, will have PC and Macintosh interfaces.

Earlier versions of the Sharp Wizard have been used in a variety of
applications. Cue, a paging company in Irvine, CA, has developed a

10

vehicle-mounted dispatching and routing system called Lapcom using Wizards. And Brooklyn Union Gas, a New York-based natural gas utility, is using Wizards with an expert system for issuing deferred payment agreements. Previously, eight representatives shared a single IBM PS/2 Model 50. For the cost of a single PS/2, all the representatives now have Sharp Wizards with the expert system on an IC card.

PoqetPad

The $1995 PoqetPad from Fujitsu Personal Systems, Inc. (formerly Poqet Computer Corp.) is a DOS-based pentop with two PCMCIA slots that does handwriting recognition. Poquet Pad, shown in Figure 10-3, has no keyboard, although you can pop up a keyboard in the software and then select keys with the pen. The PoqetPad is not aimed at the end-user market. It is rather sold to VARs (Value-Added Resellers) who add form-based software for vertical markets, such as inventory, surveys, and in-store pricing. In addition to the standard mass-storage and communications PCMCIA devices, the PoqetPad can be equipped with a bar-code reader, lightweight modems, and other I/O devices.

The Poqet Pad
Figure 10-3.

Personal Digital Assistants

The term "Personal Digital Assistant" or "PDA" seems to have been coined by Apple Chairman John Sculley to describe their new personal electronic device, the Apple Newton, but several other LTCs seem to fit the description. Hewlett-Packard calls this type of computer "mobile information appliances." GO calls them "personal communicators." Whatever they're called, manufacturers are trying to get people to think of PDAs as "an appliance rather than a tool"—they should be so natural to use that people don't think so much about using the tool, but rather the problem at hand.

The Apple Newton

The Apple Newton is the first of a line of PDAs from Apple Computer. It uses the Newt operating system, which is not Macintosh compatible. The Apple Newton, shown in Figure 10-4, comes with a name and address database, a notepad, a calendar, and e-mail capabilities. It also has a PCMCIA slot. The Apple Newton is scheduled for release in the first quarter of 1993 and is expected to sell for well under $1,000.

10

The Apple
Newton
Figure 10-4.

One of the key features of the Apple Newton (and other PDAs) is that it anticipates what you're doing and helps you to do it. For example, if you want to enter a telephone number in a standard palmtop, you need to tell it you're entering a telephone number, go to the proper field, and type the number in. Even pentops require you to write the data in a place where it can recognize it; you've just substituted the pen interface for a keyboard. Information is stored in records and files.

By contrast, the Apple Newton lets you enter information on the penpad and then makes an informed decision about what it should do with the information. If you write a phone number on the pad, the Apple Newton recognizes the string of digits as a phone number, and saves it as a phone number. If you have a name next to the number, the Apple Newton tags the name to the number. Later, you can write yourself a note that says "Call Bob." The Apple Newton recognizes "call" as an action word, and looks for the phone number associated with the next part of the statement: "Bob." If you had several Bobs in the Apple Newton already, it would display a list from which you could select the right name and number simply by tapping the right one.

Similarly, if you sketch something on the pentop, the Apple Newton will help you out. Sketch a rough circle, and the Apple Newton will display a computer-drawn circle. Draw a square, and the Apple Newton will make sure the edges are straight and the corners are all right angles. Draw a street map, and the Apple Newton will smooth out the uneven lines and pretty up the street names you wrote in.

The Apple Newton's first generation will have direct serial links and IR access, but according to Michael Spindler, Apple's president, Apple is also planning other PDAs. For example, Apple and Toshiba have teamed up to produce a CD-ROM-based PDA code-named "Sweet Pea." Other PDAs will give users wireless access to remote databases and have telephone and voice messaging.

Both the Apple Newton and the Sweet Pea will have a variety of software and information that emphasizes their value to the business traveler. Random House is publishing Fodor travel maps of various cities in Apple Newton format.

Personal Communicators: GO's PenPoint Operating System

GO's PenPoint operating system is designed for mobile pen operations. It's designed with a "pen-and-paper" metaphor—the operating system "desktop" looks just like a paper notebook, including tabs, pages, and a table of contents. To open a document, you turn to the appropriate page in the notebook. PenPoint then launches the appropriate application using the selected file. Over 50 applications designed to run on PenPoint have been announced by companies like Lotus, Oracle, Novell, and WordPerfect. PenPoint also has strong connectivity options: it supports a variety of networking environments, including Novell's NetWare, TCP/IP, and AppleTalk.

GO has teamed up with AT&T Microelectronics to design a family of products known as "Personal Communicators" based on GO's PenPoint operating system and AT&T Microelectronics' "Hobbit" architecture. No products have yet been released, but some of the products being considered are

✦ *The Travel Companion* A true PDA, this unit would be linked to a cellular phone via a standard RJ-11 jack.

✦ *The Tablet Communicator* About the size of a sheet of paper, a large pen screen lets you sketch drawings, compose or mark up faxes one page at a time, and view documents as they'd be printed. You can plug the Tablet Communicator into a phone and send and retrieve phone messages and faxes.

✦ *The Office PhonePad* This is a combination phone/voice-mail unit with a built-in PDA. You can quickly find a phone number in the PDA and dial it by tapping the name on the screen. You can take notes on the screen during the conversation, after which you can send them over the phone to another computer, a fax, or an online information service.

10

Although the PenPoint operating system is not yet widely released, there are a number of third-party PDAs planned for 1993 that use PenPoint. Samsung currently has a tablet-sized computer about the size of a sheet of paper that uses PenPoint, and EO, Inc., is planning to release a Personal Communicator pentop unit in early 1993.

LTCs, PDAs, and Connectivity

Current LTCs and PDAs let you use serial links for direct connection to modems, printers, faxes, and other devices. Running a serial cable from your LTC to an external device lets you connect to virtually anything accessible by a serial or telephone link, as shown in Figure 10-5.

Almost all of the major LTC manufacturers have teamed up with software companies to produce serially linked software that runs on a full-sized computer. An excellent example of this is Traveling Software's PC Link software for the Casio B.O.S.S. PC Link is a complete personal information manager that runs on your desktop PC. Users of the Casio B.O.S.S. will have little trouble learning how to use PC Link, as it looks like the applications in the B.O.S.S.'s ROM. You enter information on the desktop version of PC Link by typing it in or by importing it from

Serial connection affords wide connectivity to an LTC
Figure 10-5.

other files. You can then export files to your Casio B.O.S.S. using a serial cable. The process works the other way, too. You can transfer information from the Casio B.O.S.S. to your desktop PC, where you can then use the data with your favorite applications.

Interface software like PC Link makes loading information into your LTC much easier. When you're on the road, you probably won't be adding information to the LTC as much as you will be using it to look things up, schedule appointments, and make brief memoranda—all of which take a very limited number of keystrokes.

A portable e-mail package using a wireless packet-data network that doesn't need RJ-11 ports or a telephone has been announced and is in use in 50 cities. The two-pound package, produced by RAM Mobile Data (a cooperative venture of RAM Broadcast Corp. and BellSouth), includes a portable palmtop computer and a wireless sending modem, providing a link between wireless data networks and such existing e-mail systems as MCI Mail, CompuServe, AppleLink, and Internet. While a similar network, produced by ARDIS, IBM, and Motorola already exists, it is limited to intra-company use.

Hewlett-Packard and Ericsson GE Mobile Communications Wireless Division are jointly marketing a package called Viking Express, a wireless e-mail system composed of an HP 95LX and a Mobidem portable wireless modem. The Mobidem lets you send and receive information at 8K/second over the Mobitex wireless packet-switched data network operated in North America and throughout the world. Costs are competitive, too: 25 cents for a 1K e-mail file and $50 to $80 per month in line charges. The Mobidem is available in many computer superstores and retail outlets. It works with any PC that has an RS-232 serial port.

10

Anterior Technology has already expanded on the idea of portable connectivity with a two-way wireless e-mail service called RadioMail. RadioMail lets you access e-mail systems and online information services from virtually anywhere. You can stay in touch no matter where you are.

Another network is Motorola's Electronic Mail Broadcast to a Roaming Computer network, or EMBARC. EMBARC provides one-way wireless e-mail and network access designed for executives on the road and field-service personnel. Messages are sent from a PC system and transmitted by satellite to local transmission sites that rebroadcast the signal to a NewsStream receiver, a paging device connected to the HP 95LX. When a new message appears, the NewsStream receiver flashes a green light.

You can also use the NewsStream receiver to receive stock quotes by adding a small hand-held unit called a DataPulse, available from Metriplex. You can use this with an HP 95LX to not only receive stock information but track and graphically display specific stocks during the day while you're out in the field or visiting clients. The data broadcast includes all major currency prices, futures, bonds, gold, energy quotes, and major stock indexes.

Most of the new LTCs are either built around the PCMCIA standard or have a PCMCIA interface slot. This lets you add memory cards, programs on ROM, or interface units. Databook of Rochester, NY, takes advantage of this with their ThinCard Drive, a unit that lets you swap data with any other LTC that conforms to the PCMCIA standard. You plug the ThinCard Drive into the parallel drive of your desktop PC and then download information or a program into a PCMCIA card. You can then plug the card into your LTC and read the information from the card. Similarly, you can copy data to a card and then export the data through the ThinCard Drive onto your desktop PC.

File conversion and compatibility is not a large problem yet, but only because there are not a lot of LTCs in the market yet. Most LTCs can save a file in ASCII format—crude but effective. Using the serial port and a modem or null-modem cable, you can transfer files from the LTC to any other device.

IntelliLink, Inc., of Acton, MA, makes IntelliLink 2.3, a $99.95 Microsoft Windows–based product that lets you transfer information between your palmtop and a desktop PC. IntelliLink can import and export data in many formats, including dBASE, Paradox, PackRat, Ami Pro, and Word for Windows. You can use IntelliLink with the HP 95LX, the Casio B.O.S.S., the Sharp Wizard, and the Psion Series 3.

The Writing on the Wall

1982 was "the year of the laptop computer," but laptops did not become a practical reality until 1987. Many early products came and went that shaped both the market and the market's perception. It took about five years for the idea to become accepted in the marketplace and for products that met the market's expectations to appear. What are some of the directions that PDAs will take over the next five years?

According to Dick Allen, manager of communications technology in Apple's Advanced Technology Group: "By 1995, more than half of computers sold in the United States are going to be portables, and the only kind of communications that makes sense for them is wireless." In anticipation of this, Apple is trying to establish a wireless service called Data-PCS (Personal Communication Services), which would provide unlicensed transmission for applications such as wireless LANs. The appearance of this service is not yet scheduled, as the FCC must still approve Apple's petition for frequency allocation.

Apple is not the only company that thinks there's a big future in wireless communications. IBM and Motorola are producing the IBM 9075 PCradio, a mobile cellular data communications unit with fax and modem capabilities that runs on the ARDIS network, and Motorola's Iridium Project with Iridium, Inc., will use 77 low earth-orbiting satellites (LEOS) for a global telecommunications network in 1994. A LEOS-based system would provide direct communications access to any point on the globe.

Gesture recognition is already being used for many PDAs. Pen interfaces are perfect for this: selecting items is done by circling or tapping an item on the screen with the stylus. Handwriting recognition is being improved all the time, and at least one subnotebook computer has added basic voice recognition and playback.

Sooner or later, you're going to drop any hand-held computer. Hewlett-Packard has developed their Kittyhawk Personal Storage Module, a 21.4-megabyte hard disk that's shock resistant: perfect for LTCs. Other companies are researching ways to make solid-state mass storage devices, which would be cheaper and more durable. Having 50 or even 100 megabytes online in your hand won't be far in the future.

10

Desktop PCs and online information systems have demonstrated how much information there is to access; cellular phones have shown how easy it is to be on the road and stay in contact. Combining these two desires into a usable product will be the driving force behind the eventual success of PDAs.

To be successful, the first essays into the PDA market in 1993 must be quality products, and they must also sell the idea that PDAs are not "tools," but "appliances"—that is, transparent to use, so that the user can concentrate on the problem at hand, not the tool in hand. Many of the products introduced in 1993 may prove inadequate, but there are several LTCs and PDAs scheduled to come out in the next two years that are going to sell incredibly well and reshape the computer market. We'll tell you about how those successes have fared five years from now in 1998.

Hot Links

APPENDIX

Hot Links

A

USING HOT LINKS SOFTWARE: INSTALLATION AND HELP

In this appendix, you learn how to use the linking and utilities software provided on the disk included with this book. The three software programs included with this book are Desk Connect, File Manager, and LapWrite. These utilities comprise a unified solution to your laptop linking and file-management needs. Each utility includes many powerful features, but they are much more powerful when used in combination with each other.

These software programs, produced by Traveling Software, Inc., do the following:

✦ Desk Connect is a way for your computer and laptop to communicate directly without a network.

✦ File Manager is a file- and directory-management utility.

✦ LapWrite is a word processor to work with your files and view their contents.

You can use these utility programs to connect your laptop computer (or any other DOS computer) to your desktop computer. Use Desk Connect to access the drives on your laptop as if they were additional drives on your desktop computer. Then with the File Manager, exchange and manage your data and files between the two computers connected by Desk Connect. LapWrite, also included in the software package, is a word processing program, custom designed for use on your laptop.

About Desk Connect

Desk Connect is a linking utility that facilitates communications between two DOS computers. When you use Desk Connect, one computer (usually a laptop) is designated as the server. The server functions as an extension to the client, the desktop computer. When you make a Desk Connect connection, you don't control the server with its keyboard or mouse. Instead, you access the drives on the server machine from the keyboard of the client machine.

To use Desk Connect, you will need a cable that can communicate over a serial or parallel port. These cables are available from Traveling Software at (800) 343-8080. Desk Connect is discussed in further detail in Appendix B.

About File Manager

File Manager is an integrated file- and directory-management tool. The split-screen interface is easy to use. Integrated mouse support provides quick access to pull-down menus and context-sensitive help. By setting different copy options and using the commands on the File and Select menus, you can perform many advanced file-management tasks. File Manager is discussed in further detail in Appendix C.

About LapWrite

LapWrite is a handy tool to view or edit your files. LapWrite includes a number of standard editing features, such as a clipboard, search capabilities, mouse support, and printing support. LapWrite also contains several features designed especially for the laptop user—a large type mode, a word counter, and the ability to condense the display font to show 50 lines (VGA) or 43 lines (EGA) per screen instead of 25 lines. LapWrite is discussed in further detail in Appendix D.

Installation

There are two ways you can install the Hot Links software—automatically, from the Hot Links disk onto your hard disk, or manually. Either way, the Desk Connect software must be installed on both of the machines you want to connect. If you want to run Desk Connect from a floppy disk, be sure to use a copy rather than the original disk. Make a copy for safekeeping in any event.

The Hot Links disk comes with the following files:

READEME.COM
INSTALL.EXE
INSTALL.INI
DC.EXE
FM.EXE
LW.CFG
LW.FON
DCS.EXE
FM.HLP
LW.EXE
LW.HLP

A

Installing Automatically

To install the Hot Links software:

1. Place the Hot Links disk into the appropriate drive and make that drive current. For example, if the Hot Links disk is in drive B, type **B:** at the DOS prompt and press ⌜Enter⌝ to make B the current drive. The DOS prompt should now display the letter of the drive that the disk is in.

2. Type **DIR** and press ⌜Enter⌝ to obtain a directory listing. All the files just listed should be on the disk. If the source disk is missing any of the files, INSTALL will not complete.

3. Type **README** and press ⌜Enter⌝. This will display important information concerning installation that you should see before proceeding.

4. Type **INSTALL,** press ⌜Enter⌝, and follow the onscreen instructions. The installation program will ask you where you want to install the program and will suggest default options for source drive, target drive, hard disk or floppy installation, and target directory. Use the arrow keys to move the highlight to the appropriate selection to modify it. If you are installing to a hard drive, such as C, INSTALL will suggest installation in a subdirectory called HOTLINKS; if you are installing to a floppy in a different drive than the Hot Links disk, INSTALL will suggest the root directory. It is a good idea to accept the default suggestions.

NOTE: you cannot use INSTALL to install from the Hot Links disk to the same drive (A to A or C to C). If you want to do so, you must install manually (see the next section).

Press ⌜F10⌝ to continue. The installation program tells you how much disk space the Hot Links programs will need. The installation program might ask further questions at this point. Do you want it to increase your memory buffers? This depends on whether you are using a disk cache; refer to a good DOS reference. Do you want it to change the LASTDRIVE statement in your CONFIG.SYS file? If you'll be accessing other drives, you'll want your computer to recognize them; add the number of drives you expect to access to the highest letter of your current LASTDRIVE (E is the default). Do you want it to add the target directory (for example C:\HOTLINKS) to your PATH statement? If you do this, you won't have to make the directory current before using a file in it. Answer Y or N (you might want to do these things manually or not at all) to each question. Press (Enter) to continue.

Upon completion, INSTALL will inform you of installation success. Press (Esc) to get a last-minute reminder about the programs and return to the DOS prompt.

5. Make the drive (and directory, if you've installed to a hard disk) with the Hot Links programs current. If, for example, you've installed to C:\HOTLINKS, type **C:\HOTLINKS**. You are now ready to run the Hot Links software.

TIP: If you've put the HOTLINKS directory into your PATH statement, you won't have to make the drive and directory current to use the Hot Links software after the next time you start the computer.

Installing Manually

To install the Hot Links software manually:

1. Place the original disk in the appropriate floppy drive on your PC.

2. Make the drive with the Hot Links disk current. For example, if your Hot Links disk is in drive A, type **A:** and press (Enter). The DOS prompt should now display the letter of the drive that your Hot Links disk is in.

3. Copy all the files (you won't need to copy the INSTALL files) to your target disk. For example, if you want to install the software manually into the HOTLINKS directory on drive C (C:\HOTLINKS), type **COPY A:*.* C:\HOTLINKS** at the DOS prompt and press (Enter). For information about creating a HOTLINKS directory on your hard drive, see the manual for your operating system.

To copy all the files onto a target disk in the same drive (assuming drive A, for example), type **COPY A:*.* A:** at the DOS prompt and press (Enter). You will be told when to place the source disk and when to place the destination disk into the drive.

4. Since you don't need the INSTALL program in a manually installed setup, you can type (assuming a disk in drive A) **DELETE A:INSTALL.*** at the DOS prompt and press (Enter) to remove the two INSTALL files from the target disk. This is not necessary.

5. Type **README** and press (Enter) and read the information it contains.

6. If you've copied the Hot Links files to a disk in a different drive, make that drive current. If, for example, this is drive B, type **B:** and press (Enter).

When you have finished, the files listed in the previous section should be on your target disk (type **DIR** and press (Enter)). You are ready to use the Hot Links software.

TIP: If you need to conserve disk space when installing your Hot Links software on the server computer, copy only the Desk Connect Server file (DCS.EXE) to the server. You only need to run the Desk Connect Server program on the server—the rest of the files are for the client PC and for LapWrite and File Manager. If you need to save disk space on the client computer, don't copy the INSTALL programs or DCS to the client.

Getting Help for Desk Connect, LapWrite, and File Manager

All of the applications included in this package are very easy to use, but you'll be glad to know that online help is available at any time. To activate the help system for File Manager or LapWrite, press (F1) or click the Help icon (?) that appears at the top right of each pull-down menu. To activate the help system for Desk Connect, type **DC –?**.

Online instructions are available in the Help for all of the tasks and commands in each program or utility. However, if you would like to have a permanent copy of the lessons, just print them out as described in the following procedure.

To print a copy of a Help topic, press Prt Sc. For more information on using the Prt Sc key, see your DOS manual.

Getting Technical Support

Technical support for this software package is available from Traveling Software, Inc., from 8:00 A.M. to 5:00 P.M. Pacific Standard Time, at (206)483-8088.

Warranty and License Agreement

The following section details your rights and responsibilities regarding the use, distribution restrictions, and transfer of the Hot Links software.

The Traveling Software License Agreement

Each Hot Links software package is intended for use by a single user on only one pair of computers at a time. This license permits use of the Software only by the licensee, on only one pair of computers at a time and not where more than one person can use it simultaneously, including a multiuser system or network.

You may transfer the right to use this software to another person as often as you like if they agree to the terms of this license and no copies of the software licensed herein are retained for use by any other person.

The software you have purchased with this book is not copy protected, but you are free to make only one working copy of the Hot Links programs for archival purposes. Your adherence to this agreement will allow us to develop other innovative and useful products and to provide a high level of customer service and support.

Please locate the serial number of your original disk. You will need this number to receive telephone support.

A

APPENDIX

Hot Links

B

USING
DESK CONNECT

Desk Connect is useful when you don't have a network available for file exchange. Just connect the two computers with a cable and use your desktop applications to edit files on your laptop computer. For example, suppose you are using your PC and suddenly realize that the spreadsheet you need to work with is on your laptop. Connect the two with a cable and start Desk Connect. You can access your spreadsheet on the laptop from an application running on your desktop computer without having to copy files or use a floppy disk.

In this appendix, you learn how to:

✦ Start Desk Connect on the server and client

✦ Change the Desk Connect client settings under DOS

✦ Run Desk Connect while in Windows 386 Enhanced mode

✦ Use an existing network with Desk Connect

✦ Remedy common Desk Connect communication problems

The Desk Connect Program Files

The following table lists the files that are installed when you install Desk Connect.

File	Description
DC.EXE	The client PC memory-resident program (TSR). This program must be running in order to communicate with the server.
DCS.EXE	The server PC program. When started, this program takes over the server PC and makes the server's drives available to the client. (Must be copied to the server manually.)

System Requirements for Desk Connect

To run Desk Connect and connect to another PC or laptop, each computer must meet the following minimum requirements.

Hardware Requirements

The hardware requirements for Desk Connect are as follows:

✦ The PCs must be 100-percent IBM compatible (this includes machines compatible with the IBM PC, XT, AT, or PS/2).

✦ The client PC must have at least 62K of available memory .

✦ Each PC must have at least one RS-232 serial or one parallel port.

✦ You need one 9-pin or 25-pin serial connector cable or a 25-pin
parallel connector cable, available from Traveling Software at their
toll-free order line, 1-800-343-8080.

Software Requirements

To use Desk Connect, each machine needs MS-DOS or PC-DOS version
3.1 or above.

Quick Start—Desk Connect

If you're an experienced user and know which ports and connections
are available on your machines, you can use the following simple
instructions to get up and running with the Desk Connect software:

1. Connect the two computers using a serial cable. Attach the
   cable to the computers' COM1 ports.

2. On the server, copy the DCS.EXE file from the enclosed disk
   to the computer's hard drive; then type **DCS** and press (Enter)
   to start Desk Connect. The server is now ready to
   communicate with the client over the COM1 serial port.

NOTE: If you are not using COM1, you need to designate
another port with a command-line switch. For more
information, see "Starting Desk Connect on the Server."

B

3. On the client computer, copy DC.EXE from the enclosed disk
   to the computer's hard drive; then type **DC** and press (Enter).

At this point, the server is dedicated to use by the client. In other
words, you cannot run an application located on the server. A list of
mapped server drives is displayed on the client computer's screen.

You can now access the directories and files on the server as though they were located on the client. To copy, move, or delete files, use the File Manager. For information on starting and using the File Manager, see Appendix C.

Connecting PCs with a Cable

The parallel cable is always a 25-pin male-to-male cable. The serial cable is either a 9-pin or 25-pin cable, usually female-to-female; occasionally a serial port gender will differ from the norm.

Parallel ports send data over several wires of the cable simultaneously and therefore can transfer data much more quickly than serial ports. However, because most PCs have only one parallel port (and that is usually reserved for the printer connection), it may be more convenient to use a serial port.

Serial port connectors come in two sizes—DB-9 and DB-25. It is possible to have up to four serial ports, labeled COM1 through COM4. Be sure to check your hardware documentation for the correct location of the ports. Using an incorrect port may damage your computer or impede the software from making a connection.

You can get the necessary serial or parallel connector cable by contacting Traveling Software Customer Service at 1-800-343-8080.

To connect two PCs:

1. Choose either a parallel or serial connection (you must use the same type of connection on both computers). Check to be sure that both computers have available ports.

2. Connect the appropriate cable to the same type of port on both the laptop and the PC.

    A 9-pin serial connector on one machine may be connected to a 25-pin serial connector on the other. If the serial port on your computer is a female port, you'll need to purchase a gender changer before you can attach the cable.

    If you are connecting via a parallel port, do *not* use your printer cable to connect the two machines. You must use a communications cable that can support standard or accelerated mode. If you attempt to use the printer cable instead, you can damage your hardware.

NOTE: A "male" connector has pins instead of holes. Serial ports are generally male. Parallel ports are almost always "female" and have holes instead of pins.

Changing CONFIG.SYS

In DOS, you can set a LASTDRIVE statement, which determines the maximum number of drives that DOS recognizes. The statement is included in your CONFIG.SYS file, located in the root directory from which you start your PC (usually C). For example, if your CONFIG.SYS file contains the statement LASTDRIVE=M:, DOS can recognize drives A through M, but not N through Z. If CONFIG.SYS does not contain a LASTDRIVE statement, DOS only recognizes drives A through E.

To make enough drives available for Desk Connect's use on the client computer, you may need to edit or add a LASTDRIVE statement to your CONFIG.SYS file.

To change your LASTDRIVE statement:

1. Open CONFIG.SYS with LapWrite on the client computer.
2. Check CONFIG.SYS for the following statement:

   LASTDRIVE=X

   where X is the last drive letter the client computer can use.
3. Edit this line or add one if necessary. (We recommend that you use K.) Then save the file as ASCII text (or the Text-Only option) and exit the editor.

   For example, if you replace X with K, drives A through K are recognizable to DOS.
4. Restart your PC.

B

NOTE: If your PC is connected to a network, there is a good chance that the LASTDRIVE statement has already been added. For more information about Desk Connect and the network, see "Using a Network with Desk Connect."

Starting Desk Connect on the Server

To start the Desk Connect server program, type **DCS** at the DOS prompt and press Enter.

The default settings will appear on the server's screen, as shown here:

```
                     Desk Connect version 1.0
       (c) Copyright 1992 TRAVELING SOFTWARE, INC. -- All Rights Reserved


Configuration:
    Port : COM1            Address : 3F8
    Baud rate: 115200       IRQ : 4


Client drive(s) mapped to Server drive(s):
    K:==C:
    L:==D:
    N:==E:

Additional drives available on the Server:
    F:

For Help, type DC -?
```

At this point, the server is dedicated for use by the client. In other words, you can't use this machine for any other application until you exit the Desk Connect server program, DCS.EXE.

To quit the server program, press Esc. Then type **Y** to confirm that you want to end the Desk Connect session.

NOTE: You must start DCS on the server before you try to run Desk Connect on the client. Also, be sure to verify that the appropriate cable is securely fastened to each of the computers.

The following table describes the command-line switches available for controlling the way DCS.EXE communicates with the client PC. Use these switches to set different options for the program.

Switch	Values and Description
–P: (port) DCS –P:L1	C1, C2, C3, C4, L1, L2, L3. Specifies the port over which to communicate. Values C1 through C4 specify serial ports COM1 through COM4. L1 through L3 specify parallel ports LPT1 through LPT3. Usually, this is the only switch you need to use. When you select a port, Desk Connect checks the port and assigns values for the address, interrupt, and communication mode.
–A: (address) DCS –P:C2 –A:2E8	Three-character hexadecimal value. Specifies the address of the port. In most cases, you do not need to specify an address, and you can use the P switch by itself, but if you designate a port that uses a nonstandard address, you should specify the address with the A switch. Common values are 3F8=COM1, 2F8=COM2, 3E8=COM3, and 2E8=COM4 for serial ports; 3BC=LPT1, 378=LPT2, and 278=LPT3 for parallel ports. If Desk Connect cannot determine the address of a specified port, it uses these common values as its defaults.
–I: (IRQ) DCS –P:C3 –I:4	2 through 5, and 7. Serial ports only. Specifies the interrupt level for serial ports only. In most cases, you do not need to specify an interrupt level, and you can use the P switch by itself; but if you designate a serial port that uses a nonstandard interrupt, you should specify the interrupt with the I switch. Common values are IRQ4 for COM1 and COM3, and IRQ3 for COM2 and COM4. If Desk Connect cannot determine the interrupt for a specified port, it uses these common values as its defaults.

B

Switch	Values and Description
–S (standard) DCS –S	This switch needs no value or colon. Desk Connect can communicate in two modes: standard and accelerated. (For parallel ports, standard mode means four-bit communication and accelerated mode means eight-bit. For serial ports, standard mode means three-wire communication and accelerated mode means seven-wire.) Without the S switch, Desk Connect always tries to communicate in the accelerated mode, and only falls back to standard if one of the PC's ports or the cable connecting them cannot use the accelerated mode. The S switch forces the communication mode to standard. If you're using a cable purchased for Desk Connect from Traveling Software and your computer has reasonably modern ports, you probably won't need to include this switch. If, however, you're using a null-modem serial cable or if the port you're using is not designated to allow data communications in the accelerated mode, use the S switch so that communication is only attempted in the standard mode. When you use the S switch, the client PC will recognize the standard communication mode and will also operate in the standard mode.
–F (floppy) DCS –F	This switch needs no value or colon. It makes the floppy drives available for the client to use.
–? (help) DCS –?	This switch needs no value or colon. It calls a help screen, which describes the switches and their meanings.

Making Server Floppy Drives Available

You have the option of making all of the server drives, floppy drives, hard drives, and network drives, available. However, this may cause application and drive problems when the client PC attempts to access a floppy drive on the server when a floppy disk is not actually in the drive.

To alleviate this problem, the server does not automatically make its floppy drives available. If you want to use the server floppy drives, you must start the server program with the –F switch.

NOTE: If you are using a parallel cable, you may also need to unload and then reload DC.EXE on the client. To do this, quit Windows (if you are running Windows), type **DC –U** at the DOS prompt, and then type **DC.**

For example, the following command line will start the server for communications over the default (COM1) serial port *and* make the floppy drives available:

```
DCS  -F  Enter
```

You can combine other switches with –F. The following example starts the server for communications over LPT2 and makes the server floppies available:

```
DCS  -P:L2  -F  Enter
```

If you don't want to use the server floppy drives, don't include the –F switch.

Implications of the –F Switch

There are several implications to the manner in which floppies are accessed. For instance, the Desk Connect client (where you run DC.EXE) may not "see" the server floppy drives until you use the Desk Connect server application to map the floppy drives. If you previously started the server without the –F switch, you should start DCS.EXE on the server with the –F switch (as noted above).

You can save these settings for DCS.EXE in a batch (BAT) file on the server so that the next time you start Desk Connect, the floppy drives will be mapped automatically.

Next, start DC.EXE on the client. After mapping floppy drives (so that they are available to the client PC) you should, as much as possible, keep floppy disks in the server drives. This is because many Windows

B

applications might attempt to access the server floppy drives, especially when opening and saving files.

For example, if you issue the OPEN command from an application, the application may check all drive letters, including the letters for the server floppy drives. If the server floppy drive is empty, the server's floppy drives and/or the server's hard drives might not be shown in the drive list. (This is due to the fact that some applications have trouble working with network drives that have removable media. That is, some applications recognize the server floppy drives as network drives, but do not "expect" a network drive to be a removable floppy.) In other cases, if you actually click a drive letter that represents the server floppy drive you might receive an error such as, "System Error. Cannot read from drive E:. Cancel. Retry." This simply means that there is no floppy in the drive to be read.

Thus, if you map server floppy drives, try to keep a floppy in the server drive. If you don't intend to use the floppies on the server, don't use the –F switch, and they will not be available for mapping.

Starting and Using the Client from DOS

You control Desk Connect by issuing commands from the DOS command line. You can check and change its settings using many of the same commands and switches available to the server machine. You can precede the switch letters with hyphens (–) or with forward slashes (/).

To start the Desk Connect client program, type **DC** at the DOS prompt and press Enter.

In the left column, the "mapping" shows the drive letters you use to access files on the server (the client sees the drives as these letters). The default settings are COM1, baud rate=115200, accelerated (or eight-bit communication) mode.

If you are using a port other than COM1, such as COM2, be sure to designate it with the proper command-line switch when starting Desk Connect. Switches control the way Desk Connect communicates, allowing you to set different options for the program. For information about how to use them, read the following sections.

All of the command-line switches shown in the previous table for the Desk Connect server program are available for use in the Desk Connect client, with one exception: the –F switch. In addition, the following command-line switches are available for the client:

Switch	Values and Description
–B: (baud rate) DC –B:38400	115200 (default), 57600, 38400, 19200. Specifies the baud rate to use. In Windows, you might want to step down to 57,600 if you have problems communicating.
–D: (drive) DC –D:F	A through Z.* Specifies the first drive from which to begin mapping. The first drive published by the server will be known by this letter on the client.
–U: (uninstall) DC –U	This switch needs no value or colon. Removes the memory-resident Desk Connect from memory. As with all TSRs, the last one installed should be the first one removed.
*Note: The remote value won't overwrite a client computer's existing drive. If, for example, you have drives in your client computer through C installed and you specify A for the –D value, Desk Connect assigns D, the next available drive letter, to –D.	

Getting Help

To view a screen containing a list of all the DC.EXE switches and their meanings, type **DC –?**.

Displaying the Current Settings

To check the current Desk Connect settings from the DOS prompt, type **DC** and press ⌷Enter⌷.

 Desk Connect displays a message and the current settings:

✦ *Configuration* Shows the current port and baud rate, as well as technical information about the port (address, IRQ, and communication mode).

B

◆ *Client drive(s) mapped to server drive(s)* The left column shows the drive letters you use to access files on the server (the client sees the drives as these letters). The right column shows the actual drive letters for the drives on the server.

◆ *Additional drives available on the server* This lists the drives that are available on the server that are not yet mapped. To map these drives, increase the LASTDRIVE statement by the number of drives needed. For more information, see "Changing CONFIG.SYS."

Uninstalling and Reinstalling Desk Connect from DOS

Most of the time you can just ignore the Desk Connect resident portion, which runs quietly in the background. However, if you need to use all of your computer's available memory for another application, you may want to "uninstall" (unload from memory) the memory-resident program that Desk Connect loads when you start your system.

To uninstall the Desk Connect memory-resident program from the DOS prompt, type **DC –U**, and press Enter. Desk Connect displays messages if files are open on any of the server drives being used by the client.

To reinstall the Desk Connect memory-resident program from the DOS prompt, type **DC** and press Enter. Be sure to include any necessary switches to obtain the correct settings. Desk Connect displays a message and lists the current settings.

Changing the Communication Settings

The default settings of Desk Connect will be fine in most cases. If they're not compatible with your configuration, you can change them during setup or type commands at the DOS prompt. The command always begins with "DC", followed by one or more switches. The following sections discuss changing the settings.

Changing the Baud Rate

To change the baud rate of the client computer:

1. Type **DC –B:*nnnnn*,** where *nnnnn* is one of the following valid baud rates: 115,200 (the default), 57,600, 38,400, or 19,200.
2. Press Enter.

   For example, typing **DC –B:38400** changes the baud rate to 38,400.

Changing the Port

To specify a port, you use the following switches:

```
DC [-P:Cn or Ln] [-I:n] [-A:xxx] [-S]
```

where *n* is a one-digit decimal number and *xxx* is a three-digit hexadecimal address.

Use the I switch only if you are designating a serial port. The following examples show some common ways to specify a port.

If you have connected the Desk Connect cable to the COM2 serial port, start DC.EXE by typing the following:

```
DC -P:C2
```

To start the server for a parallel port, use the –P switch, specifying L1, L2, or L3 instead of C*n*. The following command starts Desk Connect and uses the LPT2 port:

```
DC -P:L2
```

If you use COM3 or COM4 and Desk Connect doesn't communicate when you use DC –P:C3 or DC –P:C4, the interrupt-level switch (–I) may be required, and it must be used with the port (–P) switch for serial ports. For example, to use COM3 with an interrupt level of 4, type

```
DC -P:C3 -I:4
```

The address switch (–A) must be used with the port (–P) switch. If you want to use address 2E8 for COM2, type

```
DC -P:C2 -A:2E8
```

B

For the fastest operation, Desk Connect is designed to be used with cables from Traveling Software, which permit an accelerated communication mode. In some cases, however, Desk Connect is unable to connect in accelerated mode. Although Desk Connect should automatically switch to standard mode, you might need to set this switch manually. If Desk Connect fails to automatically make this switch and the port in question is COM2, you would type

```
DC -P:C2 -S
```

Assigning Drives

DC.EXE always assigns all server drives to the client. However, with the –D switch you can tell Desk Connect where to begin lettering the drives.

To choose the first drive used on the client for the server drives, type **DC –D:*x***, where *x* is the drive letter you want to begin assigning server drives to.

For example, DC –D:E sets drive E as the first available client drive letter to assign server drives to. Additional drives would be assigned to F, G, H, and so forth, in sequential order.

Your LASTDRIVE statement in CONFIG.SYS must accommodate the additional server drives. For more information on editing the LASTDRIVE statement, see "Changing CONFIG.SYS," earlier in this appendix.

Changing More Than One Parameter at a Time

You can combine any number of switches in the same command line. For example, the following command sets COM2 as the Desk Connect port, sets the baud rate to 38,400, and sets drive F as the first drive letter that server drives will be assigned:

```
DC -P:C2 -B:38400 -D:F
```

Using a Batch File to Start Desk Connect on the Client

You can add all of the switches discussed in the previous section to your AUTOEXEC.BAT or another batch (BAT) file to start Desk Connect and set all the configuration options automatically.

For example, to start Desk Connect, specifying COM2 as the port to use and 38,400 as the baud rate, add the following line to a batch file:

```
DC -P:C2 -B:38400
```

When you're ready to run Desk Connect, just run the batch file, and Desk Connect will use all of the specified settings. See your DOS manual for more information about using batch files.

Troubleshooting

If, after following the instructions in this appendix, you cannot create and maintain a Desk Connect connection, check the following areas:

✦ *Tune the baud rate.* The Desk Connect client determines the baud rate for both PCs. Because some PCs (for example most IBM PS/2 models) will not maintain a connection at 115,200 baud, try setting the baud rate on the client to a lower value. You can use the –B (baud) switch from DOS. A setting of 38,400 is generally good to use if you suspect that speed is the problem.

✦ *Ensure that the Server is connected and running DCS.EXE.* The next most likely reason that a connection is not established is that the server is not running or it is not connected. Check the cable connection and start the server by typing **DCS** and pressing ⌈Enter⌋.

✦ *Make sure that both the server and client are using the correct ports.* Unless they are both using COM1, both the server and client must be told to use the ports to which the cable is connected. On both the client and the server, use the –P (port) switch.

✦ *Try using the standard communication mode.* Most recently manufactured PCs support the accelerated communication mode (eight-bit parallel or seven-wire serial communication). However, this may not be the case for both the client and the server, and together they may only be able to communicate in the standard (four-bit parallel or three-wire serial communication) mode. To change to standard mode, add the S switch to the client command line. You might need to add it to the server command line as well.

B

Utility Software and Desk Connect

Utility programs that directly access a drive's file allocation table will probably not operate on drives that have been redirected by Desk Connect. This means that you won't be able to use programs like Norton Utilities (which includes NDD, Speedisk, Diskedit, and Dirsort) and PC Tools (which includes Compress, Disktool, and Diskfix) because these programs read the file allocation table.

DOS Commands and Desk Connect

Server drives appear as network drives to the client, and DOS does not permit some commands to be used on network drives. Therefore, you cannot use the following DOS commands for Desk Connect server drives:

APPEND CHKDSK DISKCOMP DISKCOPY FASTOPEN FDISK FORMAT JOIN LABEL MOVE RECOVER SHARE SUBST SYS XCOPY

Piping and Redirection with Desk Connect

When running DC.EXE, do *not* use piping or redirection commands. The results will be unpredictable, and your system may freeze. Redirection and piping are commonly used with the MORE and SORT commands in a batch file. These commands are incompatible with Desk Connect because redirection is one of the basic functions of the product.

Using [Ctrl]-[Break]

If your client PC freezes or displays error messages when you press [Ctrl]-[Break], check the client PC's CONFIG.SYS file for a line that reads BREAK=ON. This statement causes problems for Desk Connect if you use it while the client PC is accessing a drive on the server. Unless you have a specific need for increased break checking, delete the line from the client PC's CONFIG.SYS file.

Since the BREAK=ON command can also be run from the DOS command line, check your AUTOEXEC.BAT file for the same statement.

After making changes to either CONFIG.SYS or AUTOEXEC.BAT you should restart your PC.

Using Desk Connect in 386 Enhanced Mode

If you are running Windows in 386 Enhanced mode, you should be aware of the following issues:

✦ Desk Connect must be started and establish a connection before Windows is started. This allows the server drives to appear in all applications.

✦ DCS.EXE should not be run from a DOS box, but only from the DOS prompt.

✦ If you lose your connection to the server after starting Windows, exit Windows and type **DC –U**. Then try lowering the baud rate and operating in the standard mode for communications.

✦ If you still lose your connection, modify your SYSTEM.INI file (located in the C:\WINDOWS directory). Change the line "device=*combuff" to "REM device=*combuff." This statement is located in the [386Enh] section of the SYSTEM.INI file.

✦ When using Desk Connect, you cannot open remote server files for Excel 4.0 with Windows (versions 3.0 or 3.1).

✦ You can open, but not save, remote files for Cardfile with Windows version 3.1. When you attempt to save a modified file to the server's hard drive, the connection will be broken.

B

Changing Drives and Directories While Task Switching

The 386 Enhanced mode allows for the task switching of Windows applications as well as non-Windows applications. If you are running two or more applications at once (task switching) and at least one of them is a non-Windows application, take the precaution of checking the current drive and directory before saving any of your files.

When you are task switching with at least one non-Windows application, changing to or from a server drive or directory in one application changes the current drive or directory for the other applications as well.

Assume, for example, you have opened a non-Windows word processor in a DOS window and a Windows spreadsheet. In the word processor you've just changed the directory to the one containing your document files. Since that directory will be the current directory when you switch back to the spreadsheet, be sure to use the Save As command to assign the proper drive and directory before saving your spreadsheet file. Otherwise, the Windows spreadsheet file will be saved in the same directory as your word processing files.

Using a Network with Desk Connect

If your client PC is connected to a network such as Novell or OS/2 Lan Manager, you should be aware of the interactions between Desk Connect and the network:

✦ To most applications, the Desk Connect drives appear as network drives. You need to keep track of which drives are true network drives and which are drives provided by Desk Connect.

✦ You should always start your network and set up your network drives before you start DC.EXE. This prevents Desk Connect from appropriating drive letters that you prefer to assign to true network drives. Starting Desk Connect after your network also prevents network errors that may occur if the true network will not run when other connections are previously started.

Lan Manager expects to find a LASTDRIVE =Z statement, which permits the use of drives A through Z. Novell Netware uses drives that occur after the LASTDRIVE statement—if Netware finds LASTDRIVE=E, it will use drives F through Z.

✦ The LASTDRIVE statement in your CONFIG.SYS affects the drives that can be accessed. Desk Connect cannot map drive letters that are beyond the drive specified in the LASTDRIVE statement. For example, if CONFIG.SYS contains a LASTDRIVE=M statement, you are not able to map any drive after N with Desk Connect. If you do use a LASTDRIVE statement, be sure that it allows room for the drives you want to map with Desk Connect and your network. For more information about setting the LASTDRIVE statement, see "Changing CONFIG.SYS," earlier in this appendix.

B

APPENDIX

Hot Links

USING FILE MANAGER

The File Manager (FM) is the Hot Links utility for working with directories and files on a PC. Used in combination with Desk Connect, you can easily transfer files between a laptop and your PC. When Desk Connect is running in conjunction with File Manager, the information on your laptop shows up under File Manager as additional drives on your PC.

Starting the File Manager

Once you have established a connection with Desk Connect, start the
File Manager on the client to access the drives on the server.

To start the File Manager from the DOS prompt, type **FM** and then
press Enter.

NOTE: If you didn't install the Hot Links software in a directory
included in your PATH statement, first change to the directory
containing the File Manager files before typing the command.

The contents of the current directory are shown in the left window, and
the available drives are shown in the right window. The drives on the
server are listed as network drives on the client.

The File Manager Screen

The FM screen is divided into two windows, as shown in Figure C-1.

If you highlight the Tree line near the top of the window and press
Enter, you can see a tree diagram of the current disk. You can then

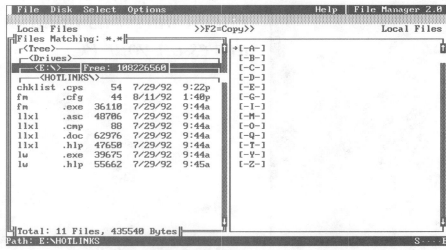

The File
Manager screen
Figure C-1.

move the highlight to a tree branch, press (Enter), and see the contents of the directory.

To copy items, select them in one window and press (F2). You can select in either the Tree mode or the file List mode.

Items are always copied from the active window (it is surrounded by double lines and contains a highlight bar) to the opposite window.

Using Help

The shortcut key for Help is (F1).

You can display the Help window at any time by pressing (F1) or clicking on the question mark (?) in the upper-right corner of a dialog box or menu.

To scroll through Help, use the (↑), (↓), (Pg Up), or (Pg Dn) keys. If you have a mouse, you can use the scroll bar at the right of the window.

Command topics in Help contain three sections:

✦ A short description of the command

✦ If the command has a dialog box, a Dialog Box Options section containing information about the choices you can make in the dialog

✦ A Notes section containing details and tips about using the command

Index of Help Topics

To display the index of Help topics, choose Index in the Help window and, when you see the index, use the arrow keys to highlight a topic. Press (Enter) or click a topic with the mouse to view that topic.

File Menu Commands

The File menu commands (except for Exit) operate on the items you select. For example, if you select a mixture of files and directories, all of these items will be deleted when you choose Delete.

The commands are briefly summarized here. For more information, see individual Help topics or highlight the command in FM and press (F1).

✦ *Copy* Ctrl-C This command copies the selected files and/or directories to the target drive or directory, using the settings in the Copy/Delete Options dialog box.

✦ *Wildcopy* Ctrl-W This command combines the selection and copy process. By specifying wildcards, you can copy all files meeting the specification with one command.

✦ *Move* Ctrl-M This command copies the selected files and/or directories to the target drive or directory, using the settings in the Copy/Delete Options dialog box, and then deletes the selected items from the source computer.

✦ *Copy Size* Ctrl-S This command displays the total size of the selected files and/or directories and the space required for them on the target drive or directory. This is useful to see if you have enough space on the target before you copy.

✦ *Delete* Ctrl-D This command deletes the selected files and/or directories.

✦ *Rename* Ctrl-R This command renames the selected files and/or directories.

✦ *View* Ctrl-V This command displays the highlighted file.

✦ *Exit* Ctrl-X This command closes File Manager.

Copy

The shortcut key for Copy is Ctrl-C *or* F2.

Use Copy to copy selected files and directories from one computer to another.

When choosing Copy, make sure that the highlight is in the source window (the window with the selected items). To select a single file or directory, highlight the name. To select multiple files, click each file with the mouse, or highlight each filename and press the Spacebar. (You can also use the commands on the Select menu.) If no file is selected, an error message reports.

When you select Copy (with a file or files properly selected), a dialog box reports the progress. Some items might not be copied, depending on the options you set with the Copy/Delete Options command.

If you have turned on the Confirm Before Copy/Move option, you'll see a Copy dialog box containing copy size information. For information about the data in this dialog box, see "Copy Size." The dialog box contains the following control buttons:

✦ *OK* closes the dialog and begins the copy process (you can also press ⌈Enter⌉). FM will attempt to copy all the selected items.

✦ *With Rename* closes the dialog and begins the copy process. For each selected item, FM displays the Rename dialog box so that you can approve or rename each file as it is copied. For more information about the With Rename dialog box, see "Confirming/Renaming Each File As You Copy."

✦ *Cancel* cancels the command.

During the copy process, FM displays a progress dialog containing a Cancel button. If you cancel, be sure to check the target computer to see which items were copied.

Copy/Delete Options

Several Copy/Delete options are available by choosing Copy/Delete Options from the Options menu. These options determine which items are copied. These options are discussed in "Copy/Delete Options" in the Options menu section.

Confirming/Renaming Each File As You Copy

If you have turned on Confirm Before Copy/Move on the Options menu, you'll see a dialog box with a With Rename button. Use With Rename to rename each file as it is copied, or to approve each file before it is copied. The following options are open to you when selecting Confirm Before Copy/Move:

✦ *Old Name* This field displays the name of the file to be copied.

✦ *New Name* Type a new name if you want to rename the file when it is copied, or leave it blank if you want to use the same name.

The With Rename box has the following control buttons:

✦ *OK* Select OK to copy the specified file and display the name of the next selected file, if any (you can also press [Enter]).

✦ *Skip* Select Skip to ignore the specified file and display the name of the next selected file (if any).

✦ *Cancel* Select Cancel (or press [Esc]) to cancel the command.

Wildcopy

The shortcut key for Wildcopy is [Ctrl]-[W].

Use the Wildcopy command to select and copy files in one step. Just choose the command, type in a filename designation, and choose OK. All files matching the designation will be copied. The file designation can contain the DOS wildcard characters ? and *.

If the Include All Subdirectories copy option is on, Wildcopy will search each subdirectory for files matching the designation and copy those files too. It will place the files into matching subdirectories on the target, creating the subdirectories if they don't yet exist.

Use the Filter field with the Wildcopy command to restrict filenames to an eight-character base name followed by an optional one- to three-character extension. The base and extension are separated by a period (.). Selecting OK closes the dialog box and begins the copy process, while Cancel cancels the command.

During the Wildcopy process, a progress dialog containing a Cancel button displays. If you cancel, be sure to check the target computer to see which items were copied.

NOTE: When using Wildcopy, the highlight must be in the source window (the window with the selected items) before choosing Wildcopy. Also, If you select files before issuing Wildcopy, the selection will be ignored during the Wildcopy process.

Copy Options

Several copy options (available by choosing Copy/Delete Options from the Options menu) determine which items are copied. These options are discussed in "Copy/Delete Options."

Move

Use Move to copy selected files and directories from one window to the other and delete the selected files in the source window. During the process, a dialog box reports the progress. Depending on the options you set with the Copy/Delete Options command, some items might not be copied.

When using Move, the highlight must be in the source window (the window with the selected items). To select a single file or directory, highlight the name. To select more than one file, click each file with the mouse, or highlight each filename and press the Spacebar. (You can also use the commands on the Select menu.)

If you turn on the Confirm Before Copy/Move option, you'll see a dialog containing move size information (see "Confirming/Renaming Each File As You Copy" for details about this box). The dialog box contains the following control buttons:

✦ *OK* closes the dialog and begins the move process (you can also press Enter).

✦ *With Rename* closes the dialog and begins the move process, displaying a dialog box at the same time so that you can approve or rename each file as it is copied.

✦ *Cancel* cancels the command (you can also press Esc).

During the move process, FM displays a progress dialog containing a Cancel button. If you cancel, be sure to check the target computer to see which items were moved.

When using Move, several Copy/Delete options are available for use in determining which items are copied. To use these options, first choose Copy/Delete Options from the Options menu. These options are discussed in "Copy/Delete Options."

Confirming/Renaming Each File As You Move

If you turn on the Confirm Before Copy/Move option, you'll see a dialog box with a With Rename button. Use With Rename to rename each file as it is moved or to approve each file before it is moved. This box is discussed in "Confirming/Renaming Each File As You Copy."

The shortcut key for Copy Size is ⌈Ctrl⌉-⌈S⌉.

Copy Size

Use Copy Size to check the size of your selection. If the Enough Copy Space field reports "Yes," the copy will fit on the target. There must be an active source and target to use the Copy Size command .

If, when using Copy Size, the Include All Subdirectories option (Copy/Delete Options dialog box) is on, FM includes the number and sizes of the files in the selected subdirectories.

NOTE: Due to technical differences in cluster size, a selection may require different amounts of space on different disks.

When you select Copy Size, the following data is reported:

✦ *Selected* This item reports the number of items directly selected. The subcategories reported here are Directories and Files. If there is no selection, the highlight is the selection. When the Include All Subdirectories copy option is on, all lower-level directories and their files are counted. When off, only the directory and its immediate files are counted.

✦ *Files In Selection That Won't Be Copied* This field shows the files that FM will not attempt to copy because of the options you set with the Copy/Delete Options command. The fields in this category are Not Newer Than File on Target, Don't Exist on Target, and Would Overwrite Read-Only Target File. Each option is tallied separately. 0 means the option is on but no files meet the criteria for exclusion. n/a means the option is not on and a tally has not been made.

✦ *Total Files That Will Be Copied* This field shows the number of selected files minus the number of files excluded in the previous three fields.

✦ *Total Bytes That Will Be Copied* This field shows the number of bytes as determined by summing the files in the Total Files That Will Be Copied field.

✦ *Bytes Required on Target* This is the amount of space the files/directories will require on the target disk. It is a function of the number of files that will be copied, their size, and the "cluster size" on the target disk.

✦ *Enough Copy Space?* This tells you if the copy will fit. This is Yes if the Free Bytes on Target field is larger than the Bytes Required on Target field, No otherwise.

NOTE: If you are copying to a floppy drive, you can proceed with a copy even when the Enough Copy Space field says No. When a floppy disk becomes full, you will be instructed to change disks.

The dialog box only contains the OK control button (you can also press (Enter)), which closes the box.

The shortcut key for Delete is (Ctrl)-(D).

Delete

Use Delete to erase selected items. Select items with the (Spacebar), mouse, or the commands on the Select menu. Of course, you should always use Delete with caution.

When you choose Delete, File Manager asks if you want to delete the number of items you've selected, at which point you will have the following options:

✦ *OK* deletes all the selected items and closes the dialog (you can also press (Enter)).

✦ *Verify* displays a dialog for each selected item, allowing you to cancel or confirm the deletion.

✦ *Cancel* cancels the command (you can also press (Esc)).

Verifying Each File Before Deleting

Use Verify in the Delete dialog box to confirm the deletion of each file before it is erased. Select Yes to erase the specified file or No to skip the specified file and go on to the next.

Rename

Use Rename to change the name of files and directories. Names for both files and directories are restricted to an eight-character base name followed by an optional one- to three-character extension. The base and extension are separated by a period (.). You cannot use wildcard characters (? or *) when renaming files.

WARNING: Use extreme caution when renaming program files (like 123.EXE) or system files (like COMMAND.COM).

The Rename dialog box has the following fields:

+ *Old Name* is the current name of the item you want to change.

+ *New Name* is the replacement name.

The Rename box has the following control options:

+ *OK* changes the name and keeps the dialog box open to change other filenames (you can also press [Enter]).

+ *Skip* skips the currently displayed name and presents the next selected item.

+ *Cancel* cancels renaming of selected items (you can also press [Esc]). Items that were renamed before canceling retain their new names.

View

Use View to display the contents of highlighted data files. Program files (those ending in EXE or COM) are not displayed. The size of the file you can view is limited by the amount of available memory. If the memory is insufficient, you will not be able to view the entire file.

When using View, lines longer than the width of the file viewing window are "wrapped" within the window.

To scroll through the displayed file, use ⬆, ⬇, Pg Up, Pg Dn, Home, or End. If you have a mouse, you can click the scroll bar at the right of the window.

NOTE: When viewing a remote file, expect the process to take slightly longer than it does with a local file, since the data must first be transferred to the local PC before it can be viewed.

Pressing Esc or selecting Cancel closes the file and returns you to the FM screen.

The shortcut key for Exit is Ctrl-X.

Exit

Use Exit to leave File Manager.

Disk Menu Commands

The Disk menu commands are designed for disk management. Two of the commands (Make Directory and Change Directory) provide DOS functionality within File Manager. The commands are briefly summarized here:

✦ *Make Directory* creates a new subdirectory within the highlighted directory (Tree mode) or open directory (List mode).

✦ *Change Directory* displays the directory you specify.

✦ *Tree mode* switches the display in the active window between Tree mode and List mode.

✦ *Synchronize* performs a two-way copy between directories so that both directories end up with the same versions of files.

Make Directory

Make Directory is used to create a new, empty directory, using the name you specify in the dialog. The new directory is created as a subdirectory of the current directory. In Tree mode, the current directory is the highlighted directory. In List mode, the current directory is the open directory.

Names for directories are restricted to an eight-character base name followed by an optional one- to three-character extension. The base and extension are separated by a period (.). (Most users do not include the period and extension.)

To use Make Directory, type the name of the new directory in the Directory field. Use `Backspace` to edit the directory name. When you have finished, select one of the control options, shown here:

+ *OK* Choose OK to create the directory and close the dialog (you can also press `Enter`).

+ *Cancel* Use Cancel to cancel the command (you can also press `Esc`).

Change Directory

Use Change Directory to display the directory you specify in the dialog box or to quickly move to another directory or disk drive. If you wish to change to a directory whose name is displayed in a window, highlight the directory name and press `Enter`.

You can also type any valid DOS path name into the Directory field. If the path exceeds the length of the text box, the text will scroll to accommodate the longer line. You can view another disk by typing **D:\PATHNAME**, where *D* is the disk letter and *PATHNAME* is the path on the new disk.

When you have finished, use one of the following controls:

+ *OK* closes the dialog and displays the specified directory (you can also press `Enter`).

+ *Cancel* cancels the command (you can also press `Esc`).

Tree Mode

The shortcut key for Tree mode is `Ctrl`-`T`.

Use the Tree mode command to switch the display in the active window between Tree and List modes. In Tree mode, File Manager displays only directories. In List mode, File Manager displays both directories and files.

Once in the Tree mode, you can highlight a directory and press Enter. Doing so will display the List mode and will open the highlighted directory.

Selecting, Copying, and Moving in the Tree Mode

Selection in the Tree mode is controlled by the Include All Subdirectories option on the Copy/Delete Options command of the Options menu. When this option is on, subdirectories are indirectly selected and marked with a + (plus) sign. When you copy or move the directory, the entire tree structure moves along with it.

When the Include All Subdirectories option is off, subdirectories are only selected if you make the selection directly, and they are marked as individually selected items. When you perform a copy or move, each subdirectory is copied separately. The subdirectory structure is lost on the target; each subdirectory becomes a directory in the open directory.

Synchronize

Use Synchronize to copy files in both directions so that both directories contain the same data and files. During synchronization, File Manager copies only newer files when it finds files with the same names, regardless of the setting displayed in the Copy/Delete Options dialog.

If you have selected Confirm Before Copy/Move, the Size dialog box will appear.

When using Synchronize, select OK to start the synchronization and close the dialog. Select Cancel to cancel the command.

NOTE: If you have sufficient space on the target computer, you can use Synchronize to back up the entire contents of the source computer by selecting its root directory and copying the contents to an appropriate directory on the target computer.

Select Menu Commands

The Select menu commands are used to quickly select files and directories. Names for both files and directories are restricted to an eight-character base name followed by an optional one- to three-character extension. The base and extension are separated by a period (.).

When using the Select menu commands, DOS wildcards are permissible. An asterisk (*) indicates any number of characters. A question mark (?) matches a single character. For example, *.DOC selects all items ending in .DOC, and ??.DOC selects items that have two characters in the base name and end with .DOC.

As with most other options in File Manager, OK closes the dialog and selects the items that match the specified criteria. Cancel cancels the command.

Select By

Use the Select By command to select files, directories, or both by specifying filenames or wildcards (? and *) in the Select Entries Matching field.

Select All

The shortcut key for Select All is Ctrl A.

Use Select All to select all the files and directories within the current directory.

Using Select All in Tree Mode

In Tree mode, this command will select all displayed directories and all files contained within those directories, including subdirectories. Selected directories that you copy will maintain their tree structure if the Include All Subdirectories option (Copy/Delete Options dialog) is turned on.

If Include All Subdirectories is turned off, selected directories will all be copied to the same directory on the target computer, and their original tree structure will be lost.

NOTE: If Include All Subdirectories is on, File Manager displays a plus sign (+) to the left of selected subdirectories. If this option is off, File Manager displays angle brackets instead.

Using Select All in List Mode

In List mode, Select All selects all the subdirectories in the open directory, but selects only the displayed files. If you have limited the display of files with the File Display Options command, Select All will select only the displayed files, not all the files in the directory. If you want to select all files, choose File Display Options from the Options menu and choose Restore Defaults before using Select All.

Select Directories

Use Select Directories to select all directories in the current directory.

Using Select Directories in Tree Mode

In Tree mode, Select Directories selects all the displayed directories and is the same as using Select All. Selected directories that you copy will maintain their tree structure if Include All Subdirectories (Copy/Delete Options dialog) is turned on.

If Include All Subdirectories is turned off, selected directories will all be copied to the same directory on the target computer, and their original tree structure will be lost.

NOTE: If Include All Subdirectories is on, FM displays a plus sign (+) to the left of selected subdirectories; if the option is off, FM displays angle brackets instead.

Select Files

The shortcut key for Select Files is Ctrl-F.

Use Select Files to select all the files (but not the subdirectories) in the current directory.

NOTE: Select Files does not work in Tree mode.

Note that Select Files selects only the displayed files. If you have limited the display of files with the File Display Options command, Select Files will select only the displayed files, not all the files in the directory. If you want to select all the files, choose File Display Options from the Options menu and choose Restore Defaults before using Select Files.

Clear Selections

Use Clear Selections to deselect all selected items. After clearing selections, you can still copy, move, or delete the single highlighted item.

To deselect items individually, highlight each item and press the `Spacebar` or click the item with the mouse.

Invert Selections

Use Invert Selections to deselect selected items and select those items not previously selected, thus reversing the selection. Both files and directories are affected.

Invert Selections is particularly useful when you want to select most, but not all, of the items in the active window. For example, if the directory contains a few program files and many data files, you can select the program files and then choose Invert Selections to select only the data files.

Reselect Copied Items

Use Reselect Copied Items after a copying, to reselect the previously selected items. This command is useful for deleting after a copy or for copying to a second destination.

To copy the same items to two different destinations, select the items and copy to the first destination. Then, choose Reselect Copied Items and copy to the second destination.

NOTE: The Move command may be used instead of a combination of the Reselect Copied Items option and Delete to transfer files and directories.

Options Menu Commands

The Options menu commands let you control the way FM displays and copies files, and let you change the colors FM uses for the screen.

The commands are briefly summarized below.

✦ *Copy/Delete Options* allows you to change settings that control how the Copy command works.

✦ *File Display Options* allows you to specify which files are displayed in the active window and to control the order in which they are listed.

✦ *Setup* changes several FM options, including the screen color, the use of a warning beep, adjustment for display flicker, and whether options are automatically saved when you exit FM.

✦ *Time/Date Format* changes the way FM displays times and dates. For times there are six possible options; for dates there are four.

Copy/Delete Options

Use Copy/Delete Options to set options that control copies, deletions, and moves.

NOTE: Any time you turn on Include All Subdirectories, the files in the subdirectories (and any sub-subdirectories) are always included in the copy.

The Copy/Delete Options are as follows:

✦ *Include All Subdirectories*   When on, if you select an individual directory, all the subdirectories in that directory are automatically selected. When off, only the directory (and the files it contains) is selected. When in Tree mode, this option determines whether subdirectories maintain their tree structure when copied (option is on) or are copied as individual directories (option is off).

✦ *Copy Newer Files Only*   When on, only newer source files are copied over files with the same names on the target computer. This prevents overwriting a newer file with an older one.

✦ *Copy Existing Files Only*   When on, FM copies only selected files that already exist on the target computer.

✦ *Confirm Before Copy/Move*   When on, FM displays a dialog so that you can approve or deny copying a file that would replace a file with the same name on the target computer.

✦ *Delete/Overwrite Read-Only Files*   When on, FM replaces read-only files with the same names on the target computer. When off, read-only items are always left unchanged.

✦ *Confirm Before Copy/Move*   When on, FM stops before each copy and lets you confirm the operation. You can then choose to copy all the selected items or rename each item as it is copied or moved. When this option is on, the same information presented by the Copy Size command is displayed.

The following are the controls for this dialog box:

✦ *OK* closes the dialog and saves the settings (you can also press `Enter`).

✦ *Restore Defaults* sets the Copy/Delete Options to their default values: all options off except for Include All Subdirectories and Confirm Before Copy/Move.

✦ *Cancel* cancels the command (you can also press `Esc`).

File Display Options

Use File Display Options to limit the display to files that match names you specify and to change the order in which the files are listed. The Display options affect both windows.

Note that when using File Display Options, directories are always listed first. Settings are saved when you exit FM.

The File Display Options are used in the following ways:

✦ *Files Matching*   To display one file, type a complete matching filename. Use wildcards (* or ?) to display several files. For example, to display all files with a DOC extension, type ***.DOC.**

✦ *Sort By*   These options determine the order in which files are listed. You can sort by Name, Extension, Date, or Size or leave your files Unsorted. Your sort order can be First to Last or Last to First. For example, to sort files from the newest to the oldest, choose Date and Last to First.

This dialog box has the following controls:

✦ *OK* closes the dialog and sorts the list (you can also press Enter).

✦ *Restore Defaults* sets the File Display Options to their default values: all files displayed, sorted by Name in First to Last (A to Z, 0 to 9) order.

✦ *Cancel* cancels the command (you can also press Esc).

Setup

Use Setup to change several FM options, including the screen color, the use of a warning beep, adjustment for display flicker, and whether options are automatically saved when you exit FM.

✦ *Display Colors*   Choose a color setting. Many hand-held and notebook computers only support the Mono/LCD setting.

✦ *Warning Beep On*   Turn this option on if you want FM to emit an audible tone when there is a program error.

✦ *Adjust for Flicker* If you have a CGA monitor and the display flickers ("has snow") turn this option on; otherwise, leave it off.

✦ *Auto-Save Option Settings* When you make changes to any option (commands on the Options menu) or use the Tree mode, FM saves the settings when you exit. It uses the settings the next time you start FM. Turn this option on if you do not want FM to notify you when it saves the settings. If the option is off, FM will display a message before it saves.

This box has the following controls:

✦ *OK* closes the dialog and uses the new settings (you can also press ⌈Enter⌉).

✦ *Cancel* cancels the command (you can also press ⌈Esc⌉).

Time/Date Format

Use Time/Date Format to change the way FM displays times and dates. For times, you can change between 12- and 24-hour display and also choose among four different formats. For dates, you can choose among four formats.

For example, by default FM shows dates with the month first and the day of the month second, such as 3/27/92. While this date format is common in the United States, European users may wish to change this format so that the day is shown first, as in 27/3/92.

✦ *12-hour* 12-hour format makes times appear with hours from 1 to 12 and uses an a or p to denote morning or evening.

✦ *24-hour* 24-hour uses 0 through 24 and does not use a or p.

✦ *Time* Choose one of four formats. Examples are shown to the right of each format. The formats change the separator character between hours and minutes.

✦ *Date* Choose one of four formats. Both the separators and month-day-year order is changed.

This box has the following controls:

◆ *OK* closes the dialog and makes the changes (you can also press Enter).

◆ *Restore defaults* sets the options to their default values: 12-hour, h:mm time format, and mm/dd/yy date format.

◆ *Cancel* cancels the command (you can also press Esc).

A P P E N D I X

Hot Links

USING LAPWRITE

LapWrite is the text processor that comes on the companion disk to this book. LapWrite is designed to maximize utility in a limited amount of disk space. It is a perfect word processor for laptop users. If you're not using a laptop, you might still find its features quite useful. For example, the ability to append selected text to a clipboard without overwriting the existing contents is rare and quite powerful. In any case, you now own LapWrite, so you should give it a try. LapWrite includes a number of standard editing features such as:

✦ A clipboard for cutting and pasting text either within a single file or between files

✦ A find (search) feature to locate specific text and find and replace for single and global replacements

✦ Full mouse support

✦ Draft printer support to quickly print files you send or receive

LapWrite also contains utilities designed specifically for the laptop user, including the following:

✦ A large-type mode, in which all text is displayed in a big, readable font

✦ A word counter, to let you know just how long a file you have created

✦ Commands for stripping and adding carriage returns, especially useful for converting to and from the simple ASCII files retrieved from electronic mail services

About Help

LapWrite offers an extensive online help system. This menu system can be easily accessed at any time for real-time information on most any topic.

Getting Help

Help with LapWrite is available to you at any time by pressing F1, pressing Alt-H, or clicking the ? icon at the top-right corner of each menu. Once you've entered the help system, choose a command from the Help menu or click the ? icon in the upper-right corner of most dialog boxes to see information on that topic. Choose Index from the Help menu to see an index of help topics and then click the Index button in the help screen. Once in the index, double-click on a topic for more information.

Moving Through Help

To scroll through Help, use ⬆, ⬇, Pg Up, or Pg Dn. You can also use a mouse to activate the scroll bar at the right of your screen.

The Help window for a command can contain three sections:

✦ A short description of the command and the menu on which it appears

✦ If the command has a series of options, a section entitled Dialog Box Options with information about the data and choices to make in the dialog box

✦ A Notes section that contains additional information about using the command

File Menu Commands

The File menu commands are used to manipulate entire files, control windows, and quit the program. You will likely make frequent and constant use of the File menu options as you work with LapWrite. All of the File menu options are discussed in the following sections.

New

Use New to clear the screen or to start a new file after completing work on another one. If you have a file open and have not made changes, you are given the opportunity to save the file before the screen is cleared.

NOTE: When using New, the clipboard is not cleared. No dialog box appears—the command is issued immediately.

D

The shortcut
key for Open
is Shift - F2

Open

Use Open to choose a file to edit or to otherwise work with an existing file. You can open any file physically located on the hand-held PC. To open a file:

1. Select a directory with the Directories box (double-click or highlight and press Enter).
2. Highlight a file in the Files box.
3. Press Enter or choose OK.

To limit the list of files that will be opened, type limiting characters in the File Name field. For example, to find all DOC files, type ***.DOC**.

NOTE: If you wish to add the contents of a file to the one you are currently working with, use Merge, not Open.

Merge: Merging an Existing File into the Current Edit

Use Merge to select a file and copy its contents into the file you are editing. Merge copies the selected file into the active window at the cursor's current location. It does not otherwise affect the selected file.

The shortcut
key for Save
is F2

Save and Save as: Saving the Active File

Use Save to save the file in the active window. Use Save as when you want to create a copy of the file under a different name or in a different directory. Also, use Save as to save a file using the With Line Breaks option.

The first time you use Save, you are presented with a dialog box to name and locate the file. You may specify whether to include or delete line breaks at this time. Once you have used the Save option on a file, the file will be automatically saved with the filename and options you specified the first time you used Save—the action is taken immediately, without a dialog box.

Use Save as to save the file in the active window. With Save as, you can specify another filename, directory location, or line-break option. Unlike Save, this command always calls up a dialog box.

NOTE: To see the line breaks in your file, select the Setup command from the Utility menu and change the Paragraph option. Use Remove Carriage Returns on the Utility menu to remove line breaks. You can remove them from the entire file or a selected portion.

Filenames are restricted to an eight-character base name followed by an optional extension of up to three characters. The base and extension are separated by a period (.).

NOTE: Since Save will save the active file, be certain, when editing two files, that the active one is the one you want to save!

The Save as Dialog Box

The Save as dialog box presents several options. Enter the name you want for the file in the File Name field. Choose the directory you want to save to from the Directory list box, and a list of files that are in that directory appears in the Files list box.

The OK option saves a file in the designated directory but does not add a carriage return (CRLF) to each line.

The With Line Breaks option saves the file, adds a carriage return (CRLF) to the end of each line, and maintains print margins.

The Cancel option lets you close the box without taking any action (you can also press [Esc]).

D

NOTE: Use With Line Breaks when you are preparing a file to transmit via modem or over an e-mail system.

The shortcut key for Edit file 2 is $\boxed{F3}$.

Edit file 2: Switching Between Two Files

LapWrite allows you to toggle between two windows. Use Edit file 1/2 to toggle between window 1 and window 2 (if file 2 is the active file, the command shows "Edit file 1"). If the Turn split screen on/off option is on, you will see both windows at once; if it is off, you see only the active window. Use the clipboard commands on the Edit menu to copy data from one window to the other.

When the Turn split screen on/off option is off, check the number in the lower-left of the screen to see which file you are editing.

The shortcut key to toggle split screen is $\boxed{Ctrl}$ $\boxed{F3}$.

Turn split screen on: Changing Between Split and Full Screen

Use Turn split screen on/off to toggle between a single large window and two half-size windows. Regardless of the mode, you can always edit two files—even if one is not visible, you can switch to its window and edit it without leaving LapWrite or losing the first window.

When the Turn split screen on/off option is off, check the number in the lower-left of the screen to see which file you are editing. The active window is indicated by the presence of the menu bar at the top of the window. To switch active windows, use Edit File 1/2.

The shortcut key for Exit is $\boxed{F10}$

Exit: Quitting or Exiting LapWrite

Use Exit to leave LapWrite. If you are editing a file that you have not saved, you are asked whether you want to save it before exiting.

Edit Menu Commands

Use the Edit menu commands to copy and move text. The commands use a *clipboard*, a memory location to which you cut or copy text. The commands are briefly summarized below. For more information, see help for individual commands.

Copy or Cut to clipboard

The shortcut key for Cut to clipboard is [Shift]-[Del].

The shortcut key for Copy to clipboard is [Ctrl]-[Ins].

Whether you choose to copy or cut text to the clipboard, your actions will be basically the same, except that one option removes the selected text from the window and one leaves it. Use Copy to clipboard to copy text from a document and store it in the clipboard. Use Cut to clipboard to delete text to the clipboard.

NOTE: Whether you copy or cut, the text you store in the clipboard replaces anything held previously in the clipboard.

To select text for copying or cutting to the clipboard, highlight the text you wish to move with the mouse or hold down the [Shift] key and use the arrow keys to highlight a block of text.

Choose the Display clipboard option to view the contents of the clipboard before pasting it into another document or otherwise removing it.

Append to clipboard

The shortcut key for Append to clipboard is [Enter]. You cannot use this shortcut when only a single character is selected.

The Edit menu's Append to clipboard option is a very effective tool if you wish to copy text from a document and add it to the end of the clipboard's contents. This option is not even available in most high-end commercial word processors—you have to go through a manual process of pasting the previous contents of the clipboard next to the new selection, copying both units, then deleting (without the clipboard) the original. LapWrite's Append to clipboard is much easier to use.

Select the text you wish to append either by highlighting it with the mouse or by holding down the [Shift] key and using the arrow keys to highlight a block of text.

D

Before actually appending text from the clipboard, consider viewing the contents of the clipboard first with the Display clipboard option found on the Edit menu.

Paste from clipboard

The shortcut key for Paste from clipboard is `Shift`-`Ins`.

Use the Paste from clipboard option on the Edit menu to copy text from the clipboard into your active document. When you select this option, the entire clipboard contents are added at the cursor's current location.

As with other LapWrite options that involve the clipboard, you would be wise to view the contents of the clipboard (using the Display clipboard option) prior to pasting its contents into your document.

Clear clipboard

Use the Edit menu's Clear clipboard option to empty the clipboard. Beware—when you clear the clipboard, you will empty its entire contents. Be sure to view the contents of the clipboard first, before using Display clipboard, to prevent unpleasant surprises.

Display clipboard

Use the Edit menu's Display clipboard option to open a scrollable window containing the clipboard text. When you are finished viewing the contents of the clipboard, press `Esc` to close the clipboard window.

The clipboard has a maximum allowable size that is directly related to the size of the document(s) you are editing. The larger the document(s), the less memory is available for the clipboard, and vice versa.

NOTE: The contents of the clipboard may be saved between LapWrite sessions. Activate this feature by choosing Setup from the Utility menu and change the Save clipboard option to Y.

The shortcut key to toggle the select mode is [F4].

Turn select mode on: Selecting Text

The Edit menu's Turn select mode on (when select mode is on, the command reads "Turn select mode off") option is used to select text for cutting, pasting, or appending to the clipboard.

The Turn select mode on (/off) option in LapWrite is probably not the simplest way to move text. Text can more easily be moved by holding down the mouse button and dragging or by holding down the [Shift] key and moving the cursor with the directional keys: [Pg Up], [Pg Dn], and the arrow keys.

However, Turn select mode on is quite useful on keyboards that have the arrow keys located on the numeric keypad. On such keyboards for example, when you press [Shift] and the [→], a 6 is produced. You can use the [Shift] method if you turn [Num Lock] on, but this is usually not convenient.

To use this command, move the cursor to the beginning or end of the text you want to select. Then, from the Edit menu, choose Turn select mode on. Finally, move the cursor through the text you wish to select.

Select mode is turned off automatically when you cut, copy, or append to the clipboard. If you want to turn it off otherwise, choose Turn select mode on a second time.

Search Menu Commands

The Search menu commands are used to find and change text in the active file. The following sections discuss each menu command option in the Search menu.

The shortcut key for Find is [F5].

Find: Searching for Text

Use Find to search for a string of characters in an active file. When selecting Find, the search will begin at the current cursor position and move toward the end of the file. The search is case insensitive—that is, the search does not depend on how words are capitalized.

To search an entire file, locate the cursor at the top of the file before issuing the find. To quickly move to the top of the file, press [Ctrl]-[Home].

D

The shortcut key for Repeat last find is ⌈Shift⌉-⌈F 5⌉.

Repeat last find

Use Repeat last find on the Search menu to search for the text you specified in your last find. When you select Repeat last find, the search begins at the current cursor position and moves toward the end of the file. As with Find, the search is case insensitive—that is, it is independent of capitalization.

The shortcut key for Change is ⌈Ctrl⌉-⌈F 5⌉.

Change: Finding and Changing Text

Use the Search menu's Change option to search for text and replace it.

NOTE: When using Change, LapWrite will find matches, no matter how you capitalize the text. For example, "Big" will find "BIG," "big," and "bIg."

When you select Change, LapWrite will search for and replace text beginning with the current cursor position. The search will move toward the end of the file.

NOTE: To make sure you replace all occurrences of a word or phrase or the like, locate the cursor at the top of the file before issuing the Change. To quickly move to the top of the file, press ⌈Ctrl⌉-⌈Home⌉.

Print Menu Commands

The Print menu commands let you print your file and preview its format. The options available to you from the Print menu include Print, View layout, Print to display, and Print settings. Each option is discussed in the sections that follow.

The shortcut
key for Print
is F6

Print: Printing the Active File

Select Print from the Print menu to print the active file according to the values you have defined in the Print settings dialog box.

LapWrite can print to either parallel or serial ports, as well as to a file. Use the Print Settings command on the Print menu to change your print settings and then choose the Print settings command from the Print menu.

NOTE: LapWrite does not support PostScript printers unless the printer directly accepts ASCII text files. To test your printer, use the DOS PRINT command.

The shortcut
key for View
layout is
Ctrl F6

View layout: Previewing the File

Select View layout from the Print menu to preview the pages of your document as they will print. View layout shows you up to three miniature pages at a time. You can also use View layout to see the number of printed pages in your document.

Press Esc to close the preview and return to editing your file.

Print to display

Use Print to display on the Print menu to quickly review the file you are editing. When you issue the Print to display command, your file will be presented from beginning to end, one screen at a time.

Print to display shows the lines of text as they will print. While printing to the display, press any key to see the next screen of text or Esc to return to editing.

Print to display can be used very effectively to view your file with a display width that is different from the margins you set for printing.

D

Print settings: Controlling Your Printer

Use Print settings to control the way your document is formatted, to control your printer when printing, and to choose a port and set communications parameters for your printer. When you select Print settings from the Print menu, a dialog box appears. You can select each item with the mouse or by pressing the quick key indicated by the highlighting. We have divided the Print settings options and their functions into four sections, as they relate to the dialog box:

First Column: Formatting Options

The first column contains options for formatting your document as follows:

✦ *Font* The Font option indicates the font size in characters per inch. When you change this setting, the left and right margins and the width of page are automatically adjusted.

✦ *Left Margin* The Left Margin sets the number of characters that text will be indented from the left edge of the paper.

✦ *Right Margin* The Right Margin sets the number of characters that text will be indented from the right edge of the paper.

NOTE: LapWrite sets margins based on the number of characters. Therefore, it is best to set your printer to use a font where all characters have the same width (a monospaced font). For most printers, the default font is monospaced with 10 characters per inch.

✦ *Width Of Page* The Width Of Page option sets the width of paper (in characters) that you will print on. When you print, line length is equal to width of paper minus the left and right margins.

NOTE: If you use a 10-character-per-inch font (the default on most printers), keep the Width Of Page setting at 85 to give you an 8.5-inch (standard) piece of paper.

◆ *Top Margin*   Top Margin sets the number of blank lines at the top of the paper before the first line.

◆ *Bottom Margin*   Bottom Margin sets the number of blank lines at the bottom of the paper.

◆ *Page Length*   Page Length sets the number of lines to print for each page. An eject is sent after each page.

◆ *Spacing*   Enter **1** for single spacing, **2** for double, and so on. To see the effect before printing, use the Print to display command.

◆ *Justify*   Justify turns justification on or off.

◆ *Net Chars/Line*   Net Chars/Line shows the resulting line length, given the three settings above (page width minus the left and right margins).

NOTE: When Net Chars/Line shows as ???, the settings are incorrect. That is, the size of the margins is greater than the width of the page, and no text would be allowed on a line. Change any of the three measurements so that at least one character is allowed per line.

Second Column: Printing Control

The second columns contain options for printer control, shown here:

◆ *Add Line Feed*   If set to Y, Add Line Feed adds a line feed to each line as it is printed (only needed for some printers).

◆ *Halt Between Pages*   Set Halt Between Pages to Y if you have a printer that must be fed individual pages.

◆ *Number Start*   Number Start sets the page number for the first page in the file.

◆ *Quick Page Number*   When set to Y, the Quick Page Number option adds a page number to each page when you print.

◆ *1st Page Printed*   Use 1st Page Printed with End Page Printed to select a range of pages to print. Type the first page number to print.

◆ *End Page Printed*   Use End Page Printed with 1st Page Printed to select a range of pages to print. Type the last page number to print.

D

✦ *Kopies* Use the Kopies option to set the number of copies that will be printed. (This begins with K because the C is already being used as a quick key for Cancel.)

✦ *Use Printer Codes* In LapWrite, you can add printer codes by pressing Ctrl-P, and, while still holding Ctrl, pressing the letter for the printer code. If your printer supports these codes, you can perform formatting such as centered or boldface text. Choose Y to use the codes. For more information on setting printer codes, see Formatting with Printer Control Codes in the Help Index.

✦ *Net Lines/Page* Net Lines/Page shows the resulting number of lines per page, given the three settings above (equal to paper length minus the top and bottom margins).

NOTE: When Net Lines/Page shows as ???, the settings are incorrect. That is, the size of the margins is greater than the length of the page and no text would be allowed on a line. Change any of the three measurements so that at least one line is allowed per page.

Third Column: Port Settings

The third column contains options for setting the output port and communications settings, shown here:

✦ *Device* The Device option lets you choose the port to which your printer is attached: LPT1, LPT2, COM1, COM2, or File. If you are using a serial port, you will need to check your printer's documentation to see if the next four fields are set correctly. For parallel ports, the settings are not used. You can also print to a file by choosing File.

✦ *Com Speed* Com Speed sets the communication speed: 300, 600, 2400, 4800, or 9600 bps.

✦ *Parity* Sets the parity: N (none), E (even), or O (odd).

✦ *Xmit Bits* Xmit Bits sets the number of data bits: 7 or 8.

✦ *Stop Bitz* Stop Bitz sets the number of stop bits: 1 or 2.

Buttons

✦ *OK* Selecting OK closes the dialog box to leave LapWrite running under the new options (you can also press Enter).

✦ *Restore Defaults* Use Restore Defaults to change the options to their preset defaults.

✦ *Save* Saves the values in LW.CFG. The saved values are used for every document unless you use the Save With File button as discussed next.

✦ *Save With File* Saves the settings as the very first line of your file. Each time you load the file, the same settings will be used.

✦ *Cancel* Use Cancel to return to your document without affecting any changes in print settings. (You can also press Esc.)

Formatting with Printer Control Codes

Most dot-matrix and HP-compatible printers support printer control codes. These codes, embedded in the text, allow you to format your text. For example, you can center text or create headers and footers. The printer control codes need to appear before and after the text you want to be formatted.

To enter a printer control code:

1. Press and continue to hold down the Ctrl key while pressing P.
2. Continue to hold down Ctrl while pressing the letter of one of the control codes in the following table.
3. Release Ctrl—the code appears in your file preceded by a ^ (caret). The effects are not seen until you print the file or use Print to Display from the Print menu.

The control codes are shown here:

Control Code	Meaning
^A*nnn*	Line spacing (*nnn* is between 1 and 250, inclusive)
^B	Boldface print

D

Control Code	Meaning
^C	Center line
^D	Double strike
^E	Elite print
^F	Footer (put at start and end of footer)
^G	Proportional print
^H	Header (put at start and end of header)
^K	Condensed print
^L	Left indent
^N*nnn*	Define page number (*nnn* is between 1 and 250)
^O	Right justification on/off (toggle)
^P	Force page break
^R	Right indent
^S	Superscript
^T	Subscript
^U	Underline
^V*nnn*	Conditional page number (*nnn* is between 1 and 250)
^W	Wide print
^X	Hanging indent
^Y	Italic print

NOTE: Your printer might not support all of these codes; check your printer's documentation for details.

Utility Menu Commands

The Utility menu contains a number of tools and options. These options include Count words, Turn large type on, Turn 43/50 lines on, Word wrap, Change case, Remove carriage returns, and Setup. Each one is discussed in one of the following sections.

The shortcut
key for
Count words
is F8.

Count words: Checking File Size

Select Count words from the Utility menu to assess the size of the active file. When you select Count words, you will see a box that contains the following:

✦ *Size* The Size field displays the number of characters in the file.

✦ *Words* The Words field displays the number of words in the file. A word is any string of characters separated by a space, carriage return, tab, or other punctuation.

✦ *Clipboard* The Clipboard field displays the size of the clipboard in number of characters.

✦ *Free* The Free field displays the amount of free memory on your computer's RAM in bytes. For LapWrite, this is the additional number of characters you can add to your file.

✦ *OK* Select the OK button to close the box.

NOTE: Journalists find Count Words helpful when supplying stories under a deadline.

The shortcut
key to toggle
between
large and
regular type
size is F7.

Turn large type on: Large or Small Characters

Use Turn large type on (this menu command reads "Turn large type off" when type is large) to toggle LapWrite's display mode. In the large type mode, LapWrite uses your screen's graphics mode and a built-in large font to display your file. This is especially useful for laptop or hand-held computers with hard-to-read screens.

NOTE: In the split-screen mode, you can display one window with large type and the other with small.

D

The shortcut
key for Turn
43/50 lines
on is
[Shift]-[F7].

Turn 43/50 lines on: More Lines with VGA and EGA Monitors

The Turn 43/50 lines on (this reads "off" when the option is currently selected) is a particularly useful feature of LapWrite, whether you are using the program on a laptop or desktop. Use Turn 43/50 lines on (/off) if you are using a VGA or EGA monitor and you wish to display more than 25 lines on your monitor. VGA supports 50 lines and EGA supports 43.

NOTE: When you are displaying 43 or 50 lines, the display margins are still dictated by the Word wrap command on the Utility menu.

Word wrap: Controlling Display Width

Use the Utility menu's Word wrap option to change the way your files are displayed on screen. Word wrap toggles the screen display into one of three modes as follows:

✦ *At Screen Width* LapWrite starts a new line after reaching the edge of your monitor (usually 78 characters).

✦ *At Print Width* LapWrite wraps lines as they will print. Line length is determined by the Set Margins command on the Utility menu.

✦ *At Column 250* LapWrite will scroll to the right until column 250. Most lines are shown exactly as you type them; a new line is not started until you press [Enter], thus adding a hard return to the file.

NOTE: When you use Save With Line Breaks, LapWrite adds a carriage return at the end of the line as it will print. For this reason, most people will want to set Word wrap to At Print Width. Then, the displayed line length will always equal the printed line length.

To see the hard returns in your file, choose the Setup command from the Utility menu and change the Paragraph field.

Change case of selected text

Use Change case of selected text to change selected text between Upper, Lower, and Opposite case. When you select Change case of selected text, a box appears with the following choices:

✦ *Upper* Choosing Upper changes all characters in the string to uppercase characters.

✦ *Lower* Choosing Lower changes all characters in the selected string to lowercase.

✦ *Opposite* Choosing Opposite reverses the case of the selected characters.

✦ *Cancel* Cancels the command (you can also press ⌜Esc⌝).

To select text, highlight the text with the mouse or hold down the ⌜Shift⌝ key and move the cursor. You can also use Turn select mode on (or off) from the Edit menu.

NOTE: Change Case is particularly useful when you have mistakenly turned Caps Lock on.

Remove carriage returns

Use Remove carriage returns to remove carriage returns (also known as CRLFs, paragraph markers, or hard returns) from an entire file or portions of a file that you have selected.

For example, when you open most ASCII files, there is a carriage return at the end of each line, and paragraphs will not "flow" properly between the LapWrite margins. If you remove the carriage returns, consecutive lines are converted to one long paragraph, which fits smoothly between the margins.

D

Returns are not removed in the following cases:

✦ There are two returns in a row (since two returns usually separate paragraphs).

✦ The next line starts with a space or a tab character (since this indentation is usually a deliberate separation from the previous paragraph).

The following options are available with Remove carriage returns:

✦ *All*   If you select All, carriage returns are removed throughout the file.

✦ *Selected*   When you choose Selected, carriage returns are removed only from the selected text.

✦ *Cancel*   Choosing Cancel (or pressing Esc) cancels the command.

NOTE: To reverse the effects of Remove carriage returns, save the file and specify With Line Breaks. Returns will be added to the end of each formatted line.

Setup: Changing LapWrite Options

Setup lets you set several LapWrite options, including the number of characters used for tabs, sound, display colors, CRLF display, character size, whether or not the clipboard is saved when you quit LapWrite, and which key drops down the LapWrite menus. When you choose Setup from the Utility menu to change LapWrite's setup options, the Setup dialog box appears. Click each option or press the highlighted key to select it, and press or click again to toggle between the possible values for that option. The setup options and their functions are as follows:

✦ *Tabs*   Tabs sets the location of tab stops for all documents. Multiples of the number are used for additional stops. For example, if you specify 5, tabs will be set for 5, 10, 15, and so on.

✦ *Beep*   The Beep option turns the warning beep on or off. The beep sounds when there is a LapWrite error.

✦ *Save Clipboard* The Save Clipboard option lets you choose whether or not to save the clipboard between sessions. When this is on, the clipboard is saved when you quit LapWrite. A file called LW.CLP is saved in the directory where the program files are located.

✦ *Paragraph* The Paragraph option lets you pick the character that shows a carriage return (CRLF).

NOTE: As shipped, the Paragraph value is blank. When formatting and changing display modes, it is easier to see CRLFs if you make a visible selection.

✦ *Auto File Save* When enabled, the Auto File Save option automatically saves your file every ten seconds after no keyboard activity, without using the Save command.

✦ *Display Color* The Display Color option lets you choose from several color schemes, including one for LCD/monochrome monitors.

NOTE: If you have a monochrome or LCD screen, it is best to use the Monochrome/LCD setting for Display Color. Otherwise, some screen highlighting might disappear from the display.

✦ *Start-up Type Size* You can set the mode that LapWrite Type will start-up in with the Start-up Type Size option: Regular (25 lines per screen), Large (same as turning large type on), and 43/50 (same as turning the 43/50 line mode on).

✦ *Word Wrap* Word Wrap toggles the screen display into one of three modes: Screen (LapWrite starts a new line after reaching the edge of your monitor, usually 78 characters), Print (LapWrite wraps lines as they will print), and Col. 250 (LapWrite will scroll to the right until column 250).

D

✦ *Menu Hot Key*   The Menu Hot Key option determines the key you press to display a LapWrite menu. You can choose both ⌷Alt⌷ and ⌷Esc⌷, ⌷Alt⌷ only, or ⌷Esc⌷ only.

✦ *Adjust for Display Flicker*   You can control the "snow" problem often encountered with CGA monitors by choosing the Adjust for Display Flicker option. If your screen is CGA or monochrome, you might get better results with this option on.

✦ *OK*   Select OK (or press ⌷Enter⌷) to close the dialog and leave LapWrite running under the new options.

✦ *Restore Defaults*   Choose Restore Defaults to change the options to their factory defaults.

✦ *Save Settings*   Use Save Settings to save the values to a file called LW.CFG. The next time you start LapWrite, the saved values are used.

✦ *Cancel*   Select cancel (or press ⌷Esc⌷) to close the box without applying any of the new settings.

Words Menu Commands

The Words menu lets you spell-check a word, selected text, or your entire document. It also provides you with a thesaurus to help you find the exact word you need.

NOTE: LapWrite's Dictionary and Thesaurus are not included on the Hot Links disk. You will receive these files for FREE, however, simply by returning the reply card in the back of this book.

Spell-Checking Options

Use the Words menu options to spell-check a file as follows:

The shortcut key for Check Document is .

✦ *Check Document*   Check Document checks the spelling of the entire active document.

✦ *Check Selection*   Check Selection checks the selected text.

The shortcut key for Check Word is Ctrl - F9.

✦ *Check Word* Check Word checks the word in which the cursor is located.

When you choose any of the three spell-checking commands, checking begins immediately and progresses from the beginning of the file. If LapWrite finds what it thinks is a misspelled word, a list of alternatives is displayed. LapWrite shows a list of words that sound like or are spelled similarly to the word in question. If you wish to select one of the alternatives from the displayed list, move the highlight with the arrow keys to select a word and then press Enter. Press Esc to return to your document without taking any action.

NOTE: To save time when checking the spelling of your document, use Check Selected Text if you have only changed a small portion of a document, and remember that if a portion of a word is highlighted, it might show as being misspelled.

Thesaurus: Finding a Synonym

Choose the Thesaurus command from the Words menu to find a synonym—a word that has a similar meaning—for the word on which the cursor is currently located.

When you select Thesaurus in this manner, LapWrite responds with a list of words that have the same or similar meaning as the current word.

Scroll through the list with the arrow keys or the mouse to find a word that appeals to you as a replacement for the current word. Then, select one of the following options from the screen:

✦ *OK* Selecting OK replaces the word with the selected alternative.

✦ *Change All* Selecting Change All replaces all occurrences of the word with the selected alternative.

✦ *Cancel* Selecting Cancel returns you to the document without taking any action.

D

APPENDIX

Hot Links

E RESOURCE DIRECTORY

This appendix lists the names, addresses, and phone numbers of the companies mentioned in this book, along with a brief description of their products. These aren't the only companies that produce good products for linking, and this appendix does not imply an endorsement of these companies. The linking field is large, and new companies are starting up every day. Still, this will give you a good starting point in your search for the missing link.

Advanced Electronic Support Products, Inc.
1810 N.E. 144th Street
N. Miami, FL 33181
305-944-7710
LAN cables, connectors, and supplies

Allied Technology Corp.
770 Haunted Lane
Bensalem, PA 19020
215-639-0300
Data switches, cables, and print buffers

Analog Devices, Inc.
Three Technology Way; P. O. Box 9106
Norwood, MA 02062-9106
617-329-4700
Wireless links and modems

Apple Computer Corp.
20525 Mariani Ave.
Cupertino, CA 95014
408-996-1010
Macintosh computers, AppleTalk
networks, and Apple File Exchange
software

Applied Creative Technology, Inc.
8333 Douglas Ave, Ste. 700
Dallas, TX 75225
214-739-4200
Systemizer hardware-based zero-slot LANs

ARDIS
300 Knightsbridge Pkwy.
Lincolnshire, IL 60069
708-913-1215
Packet-radio public networks

Arnet Corp.
618 Grassmere Park Drive, Ste. 6
Nashville, TN 37211
615-834-8000
Multiport serial boards

Artisoft, Inc.
691 E. River Road
Tucson, AZ 85704
602-293-4000
LANtastic LAN operating system,
proprietary Ethernet cards, and laptop
LAN interfaces

Asanté Technologies, Inc.
404 Tasman Drive
Sunnyvale, CA 94089
408-752-8388
Macintosh LANs

ASP Computer Products, Inc.
160 San Gabriel Drive
Sunnyvale, CA 94086
408-746-2965
Printer-sharing solutions

AT&T Microelectronics
Dept. 52 AL 040400
555 Union Blvd.
Allentown, PA 18103
800-372-2447
Modems, packet systems, networks, and
operating systems

Attachmate Corp.
1323 S.E. 36th St.
Bellevue, WA 98006
206-644-4010
PC-to-mainframe connectivity products

Banyan Systems, Inc.
120 Flanders Rd.
Westborough, MA 01581
508-898-1000
LAN network operating system (VINES),
adapter cards, and LAN supplies

Belkin Components
1303 Walnut Parkway
Compton, CA 90220
310-898-1100
Data switches, printer-sharing devices,
LAN cables and supplies, and Macintosh
networking devices

BICC Data Networks, Inc.
1800 W. Park Dr.
Westborough, MA 01581
508-898-2422
Infrared wireless LAN

Boca Research, Inc.
6413 Congress Ave.
Boca Raton, FL 33487
407-997-6227
Modems and fax modems

Cables To Go
26 W. Nottingham
Dayton, OH 45405
800-826-7904
LAN cables and custom switching devices

Canon U.S.A., Inc.
1 Canon Plaza
Lake Success, NY 10042-1113
516-488-6700
AI Note pen-based computers

Cardinal Technologies, Inc.
1927 Freedom Road
Lancaster, PA 17601
800-233-0187
Modems

Casio, Inc.
570 Mt. Pleasant Ave.
Dover, NJ 07801
201-361-5400
Personal Digital Assistants

Central Point Software, Inc.
15220 N.W. Greenbrier Pkwy. #200
Beaverton, OR 97006-9938
503-690-8090
Deluxe option board, which allows a PC
to read Mac disks

Chic Technology Corp.
1004 K Street N.E.
Auburn, WA 98002
206-833-4836
Data Switches

Clark Development Company, Inc.
6000 S. Fashion Blvd.
Murray, UT 84107
801-261-1686
PC Board BBS software

CNET Technology, Inc.
2199 Zanker Road
San Jose, CA 95131
408-954-8000
LAN supplies: cards, cables, and hubs

Codenoll Technology Corp.
1086 N. Broadway
Yonkers, NY 10701
914-965-6300
Fiber-optic LAN cards, cables, and
supplies

Compaq Computer Corp.
P.O. Box 692000
Houston, TX 77269-2000
713-370-0670
Laptops, notebook computers, docking
stations, and desktop PC LAN servers

Computone Corp.
1100 Northmeadow Parkway, Ste. 150
Roswell, GA 30076
404-475-2725
Serial cables, ports, and concentrators,
terminal-emulation software, and
network fax software

Corollary, Inc.
2802 Kelvin Ave.
Irvine, CA 92714
714-250-4040
Ethernet modem servers

CPU Products
301 River Street
Darby, KS 67037
316-788-3749
Cables, gender changers, and adapters

Custom Computer Cable, Inc.
7161 Shady Oak Road
Eden Prairie, MN 55344
612-941-5651
Custom cables and networking products

Danpex Corp.
1580 Old Oakland Road, Ste. C112
San Jose, CA 95131
408-437-7557
LAN adapters, concentrators,
transceivers, repeaters, cables, hubs, and
IBM 3270–emulation products

DataLux Corp.
2836 Cessna Drive
Winchester, VA 22160
703-662-1500
Diskless LAN workstations

Datastorm Technologies, Inc.
3212 Lemone Industrial Blvd.
Columbia, MO 65201
314-443-3282
ProCom Plus terminal-emulation
software

Dauphin Technology, Inc.
1125 E. St. Charles Road
Lombard, IL 60148
708-627-4004
Laptop computers, laptop modems and
adapter cards, and pen-based computers

DFM Systems, Inc.
1601 48th Street
West Des Moines, IA 50265
515-225-6744
Multimode pen-based, notebook, and
desktop computer, the
TraveLite—docking station optional

DigiBoard
6400 Flying Cloud Drive
Eden Prairie, MN 55344
612-943-9020
Multiport communications cards

Digicom Systems, Inc.
188 Topaz Street
Milpitas, CA 95035
408-262-1277
Data and fax modems

Digital Communications Associate
1000 Alderman Dr.
Alpharetta, GA 30202
404-442-4000
Crosstalk terminal-emulation software

Epson America, Inc., Epson OEM
3415 Kashiwa St.
Torrance, CA 90505
310-534-4500
Laptop, notebook computers, docking
stations, pocket LAN adapters, and
modems

Enable Software
313 Ushers Road
Ballston Lake, NY 12019
518-877-8600
Electronic mail and workgroup software

First Access, Inc.
4579 Laclede Ave., Ste. 175
St. Louis, MO 63108
314-367-0451
FAX Courier software, sends faxes over
ordinary data modems via AT&T service
bureau

First International Computer of
   America, Inc.
30077 Ahern Ave.
Union City, CA 94587
510-475-7885
Notebook computers

Fountain Technologies, Inc.
50 Randolph Road
Somerset, NJ 08873
908-563-4800
Notebook and file-server computers

Fujitsu America, Inc.
Computer Products Group
3055 Orchard Dr.
San Jose, CA 95134
408-432-1300
PoqetPad and PoqetPC computers and
Poqet Computer RAM cards

Futurus Corp.
211 Perimeter Center Parkway, Ste. 910
Atlanta, GA 30346
404-392-7979
LAN-based electronic mail and
workgroup software and Team Remote
remote-access software

Galacticomm, Inc.
4101 S.W. 47th Ave., #101
Fort Lauderdale, FL 33314
305-583-5990
The Major(tm) BBS software

Gandalf Premier
1023 S. Wheeling Road
Wheeling, IL 60090
708-541-6060
LANLine 5500 remote LAN access
device, LAN hubs, and modems

GRiD Systems Corp.
47211 Lakeview Blvd.
Fremont, CA 94538
510-656-4700
Pen-based computers, laptops,
notebooks, and desktops

GVC Technologies, Inc.
99 Demarest Road
Sparta, NJ 07871
201-579-3630
Modems, fax modems, Ethernet
adapters, concentrators, and transceivers

Hayes Microcomputer Products, Inc.
P. O. Box 105203
Atlanta, GA 30348
404-840-9200
Modems and communication software

Hewlett-Packard
19310 Pruneridge Ave.
Cupertino, CA 95014
800-752-0900
Palmtop computer, LAN workstations,
servers, and peripherals

IBM Corp. ESD
11400 Burnet Road
Austin, TX 78758
512-823-7049
Token-Ring LAN, laptop computers

Identity Systems Technology
1347 Exchange Drive
Richardson, TX 75081
214-235-3330
LAN adapters, notebook computers

Image Communications
6 Caesar Place
Moonachie, NJ 07074
201-935-8880
Data and fax modems, 16550 UART
serial port boards

Inforite Corp.
1670 S. Amphlett Blvd., Ste. 201
San Mateo, CA 94402
415-571-8766
Hand-held, pen-based, data-collection
terminals with RS-232C port for data
transfer to PCs

Infralink of America, Inc.
1925 N. Lynn St., #703
Arlington, VA 22209
703-522-4412
Wireless printer-sharing devices

Interex Computer Products
2971 S. Madison
Wichita, KS 67216
316-524-4747
Cables, connectors, gender changer, and
data switches

Knozall Systems, Inc.
375 E. Elliott Road, Ste. 10
Chandler, AZ 85226
800-333-8698
Novell NetWare file management and
LAN performance analysis software

Kyocera Electronics, Inc.
100 Randolph Road
Somerset, NJ 08875
908-560-3400
Ethernet and Token-Ring adapter cards

Leading Edge Products, Inc.
117 Flanders Road
Westborough, MA 01581
508-836-4800
Laptop computers

Leviton Manufacturing, Inc., Telcom Div.
2222 222nd St. N.E.
Bothell, WA 98021
206-486-2222
Data communications cabling products
and test instruments

Librex Computer Systems, Inc.
1731 Technology Drive, Ste. 700
San Jose, CA 95110
408-441-8500
Portable computers

Longshine Microsystems, Inc.
10400-9 Pioneer Blvd.
Santa Fe Springs, CA 90670
310-903-0899
Multiport I/O cards, Ethernet and
Token-Ring adapters, PC-to-mainframe
terminal-emulation cards, notebook,
desktop, and LAN workstation computers

Max Group Corp.
201 Charles Street
Hackensack, NJ 07601
201-343-0092
ARCnet, Ethernet hubs and transceivers

Microcom, Inc.
500 River Ridge Dr.
Norwood, MA 02062
617-551-1000
Fax/data modems and
terminal-emulation software

Micro Connections, Inc.
31 Commercial Street
Plainview, NY 11803
516-933-1400
Parallel and serial cables, coaxial and
custom cables, gender changers,
serial/parallel converters, print buffers,
and laptop modems

Microplex Systems Ltd.
265 E. First Ave.
Vancouver, BC V5T 1A7
604-875-1461
LAN printer adapters

Microsoft Corp.
One Microsoft Way
Redmond, WA 98052-6399
206-882-8080
LAN manager network operating system
and electronic-mail software

MicroStar Computers, Inc.
35 Cotters Lane, Bldg. C-1
East Brunswick, NJ 08816
908-651-8686
Notebook computers

Mod-Tap
P. O. Box 706
Harvard, MA 01451
508-772-5630
LAN cabling systems

Monterey Electronics, Inc.
2365 Paragon Drive, Unit D
San Jose, CA 95131
408-437-5496
Notebook computers

Moses Computers, Inc.
15466 Los Gatos Blvd., Ste. 201
Los Gatos, CA 95032
408-358-1550
Peer-to-peer LAN systems and portable
LAN adapters

Motorola, Inc. Radio-Telephone Systems
   Group
1301 E. Algonquin Rd.
Schaumburg, IL 60196
708-590-5000
Radio wireless LAN

Multi-Tech Systems, Inc.
2205 Woodale Drive
Mounds View, MN 55112
612-785-3500
Modems, fax modems, LAN interface
cards, IBM PC-to-mainframe cards, and
multiport I/O cards

Mustang Software, Inc.
915 17th St.
Bakersfield, CA 93301
805-395-0223
Qmodem terminal-emulation software
and Wildcat! BBS software

NCR Corp.
1700 S. Patterson Blvd.
Dayton, OH 45479
513-445-5000
Notebook computers and wireless LAN

NET-Source, Inc.
1265 El Camino Real, Ste. 101
Santa Clara, CA 95050
408-246-6679
Silvernet-OS peer-to-peer LAN operating
system

Norton-Lambert Corp.
P.O. Box 4085
Santa Barbara, CA 93140
805-964-6767
Remote-control software

Novell, Inc.
122 East 1700
South Provo, UT 84606
801-429-7000
NetWare LAN operating systems

Olicom USA, Inc.
900 E. Park Blvd., Ste. 180
Plano, TX 75074
214-680-8131
Token-Ring LAN adapters and cabling
components

OpenConnect Systems
2033 Chennault Drive
Carollton, TX 75006
214-490-4090
PC-to-mainframe linking solutions

Photonics Corp.
200 E. Hacienda Ave.
Campbell, CA 95008
408-370-3033
Infrared wireless LANs

Poqet Computer Corp.
see Fujitsu America, Inc.

Protec Microsystems, Inc.
297 Labrosse
Pointe Claire, PQ H9R 1A3
514-630-5832
Data switches, parallel port extenders,
peripheral sharing devices, and e-mail
and file-transfer software

Proxim, Inc.
295 N. Bernado Ave.
Mountain View, CA 94043
415-960-1630
RangeLAN family of wireless LAN
products for desktop, notebook, and
pen-based computers

QuickComm, Inc.
2290 Ringwood Ave., Ste. K
San Jose, CA 95131
408-956-9145
Data and fax modems

QVS, Inc.
9844 Harrison
Romulus, MI 48174
313-946-1120
Cables, print buffers, peripheral-sharing
devices, and data switches

RAM Mobile Data, Inc.
10 Woodbridge Center Dr.
Woodbridge, NJ 07095
908-602-5516
Packet-radio public networks

Rose Electronics
10850 Wilcrest Drive
Houston, TX 77099
713-933-7673
Printer and peripheral-sharing solutions

Samsung Electronics America
301 Nayhil Street
Saddlebrook, NJ 07662
201-587-9600
Notebook computers

Sharp Electronics Corp.
Sharp Plaza
Mahwah, NJ 07430
201-529-8200
Sharp Wizard little tiny computers and
peripherals

SkyTel
1350 I St. N.W., Ste. 1100
Washington, DC 20005
202-408-7444
Digital pagers and wireless e-mail systems

Sony Corporation
3 Paragon Dr.
Montvale, NJ 07645
201-930-1000
PTC 500 pen-based computers

Star Gate Technologies, Inc.
29300 Aurora Road
Solon, OH 44139
216-349-1860
Multiport serial cards and fiber-optic
graphics-communication systems

Surgex, Inc.
20160 Paseo Del Prado, Ste. F
Walnut, CA 91789
714-598-5616
Cables and switch boxes

Syntel Communications, Inc.
145 Baron Lane
East Brunswick, NJ 08816
908-651-0415
Pocket fax/data modems

Systems Strategies, Inc.
One Penn Plaza
New York, NY 10119
212-279-8400
Communications software for PC-Mac
and PC-Mainframe solutions

Tatung Co. of America, Inc.
2850 El Presidio Street
Long Beach, CA 90810
310-637-2105
Diskless workstations and other LAN
hardware

Telebit Corp.
1315 Chesapeake Terrace
Sunnyvale, CA 94089
408-734-4333
Data modems

Texas Instruments Peripheral Products Div.
P. O. Box 202230
Austin, TX 78720
800-527-3500
Notebook computers

Toshiba America Information Systems, Inc.
9740 Irvine Blvd.
Irvine, CA 92718
714-583-3000
Notebook, laptop, and portable
computers

Traveling Software, Inc.
18702 N. Creek Parkway
Bothell, WA 98011
206-483-8088
LapLink Pro, MacLink file-transfer software, WinConnect disk-sharing software, and Hot Links software

UDA Motorola
5000 Bradford Drive
Huntsville, AL 35805
205-430-8000
LanFast DM20 network modems, other modems, and data comm products

U.S. Robotics, Inc.
8100 McCormick Blvd.
Skokie, IL 60076
708-982-5010
Fax, data, and LAN-server modems

Xircom Corp.
26025 Mureau Road
Calabasas, CA 91302
818-878-7600
Laptop-to-LAN and laptop-to-desktop solutions, peer-to-peer LANs, and parallel-port multiplexors

Zenith Data Systems
2150 E. Lake Cook Road
Buffalo Grove, IL 60089
708-808-5000
Desktop, portable, and laptop computers

Zoom Telephonics, Inc.
207 South Street
Boston, MA 02111
617-423-1072
Modems

INDEX

C

HOT LINKS PRODUCTS & ACCESSORIES

TRAVELING SOFTWARE

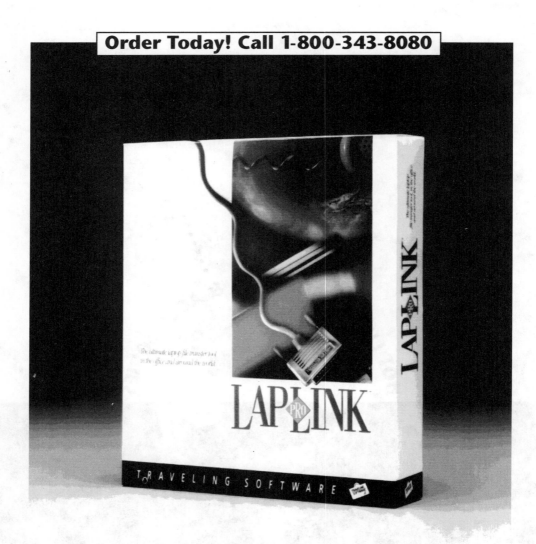

Battery Watch Pro
for DOS and Windows

Battery Watch's pop-up fuel gauge displays the time remaining on your laptop battery. Set up to 3 alarms that automatically pop up a warning. Deep Discharge helps extend the life of your battery. Works in DOS or Windows. Requires just 6-14K of RAM.

only $29.95 Sugg. Retail $49.95

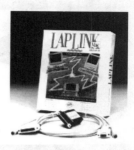

LapLink Mac III

Handle any Mac-to-Mac and Mac-to-PC file transfers with LapLink Mac. Choose the way you want to transfer files: with the included cable, via modem, over AppleTalk cables, or with a SCSI cable. You can control the file transfer from either a PC or Mac. A sophisticated password system protects your files.

only $99.95 Sugg. Retail $169.95

Order Today! Call 1-800-343-8080

CASIO PC-Link

CASIO PC-Link has everything you need to transfer data between your PC and your CASIO B.O.S.S. unit. Includes cable and powerful software that organizes your telephone directories, coordinates your schedule and reminds you of appointments. CASIO PC-Link helps you keep your PC and CASIO B.O.S.S. up-to-date.

only $99.95 Sugg. Retail $129.95

DeskLink

DeskLink connects two computers for sharing a printer or files. And it works completely in the background. A pop-up Talk Box sends messages between computers. Great for small offices. Comes complete with serial connectors and cables.

only $99.95 Sugg. Retail $169.95

Parallel Port [Multiplexor]
by Xircom

The Xircom Parallel Port Multiplexor turns one
parallel port into two. You can use both your printer
and either DeskConnect or LapLink Pro without
plugging and unplugging parallel cables.

only $89.95

Need to hook up your modem, but an RJ11 jack is
unavailable? This acoustic coupler connects to the phone
handset, instead of the jack. Works on analog or digital
systems, as well as on pay phones. Provides convenient,
reliable modem connections up to 2400 baud.

only $149.95

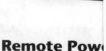

Remote Powe[r]
by Server Technol[ogies]

Control your PC anytime
On/Off. It lets you turn yo[ur]
devices on, with just a p[...]
control unit also prevent[...]

only $[...]

[...] by CP

[...]ss virtually any
[...], try the Road
[...] extension cords,
[...] adapters and
[...]ections.

DeskConnect
25-Foot Serial Cable

This extra long serial cable comes in handy when your computers are some distance apart. It comes with both 9- and 25-pin adapters.

only $29.95

DeskConnect
8-Foot Parallel Cable

This parallel cable provides lightning quick file access with DeskConnect. Speed up file access, file management and file transfer operations by as much as 100% over serial connection.

DeskConnect
8-Foot Serial Cable

Simply connect this serial cable between your laptop and desktop and access the files you want instantly with DeskConnect. This versatile, 4-headed cable works with any serial port.

only $19.95 each

Please tear at perforation and mail.

ORDER FORM

ITEM DESCRIPTION	QTY	PRICE	TOTALS
LapLink Pro		$99.95	
Battery Watch Pro		$29.95	
LapLink Mac III		$99.95	
CASIO PC-Link		$99.95	
DeskLink		$99.95	
Parallel Port Multiplexor		$89.95	
Acoustic Coupler		$149.95	
Remote Power-On/Off		$169.95	
Road Warrior Toolkit		$49.95	
25-foot Serial Cable		$29.95	
8-foot Parallel Cable		$19.95	
8-foot Serial Cable		$19.95	
SubTotal			
Sales Tax WA - 8.2%, VA - 4.5%, NY - 8%			
Shipping/Handling (2-day shipping)	.		$ 7.00
TOTAL			$

Order Now! Call 1-800-343-8080

Mon-Fri, 7am-5pm, Pacific Time

Fax order to: 206-485-6786

Mail order to: Traveling Software, Inc.
18702 North Creek Pkwy.
Bothell, WA 98011-8019

Enclosed is a check/money order in the amount of $_____

Please charge my:
☐ MasterCard   ☐ Discover
☐ VISA   ☐ American Express

Card No: _____ Exp.Date: _____

Signature _____

Name _____

Delivery Address _____

Apt. or Suite # _____

City, State, Zip _____

Day Phone (   ) _____

Evening Phone (   ) _____

LOOK INSIDE FOR SPECIAL OFFER ON HOT LINKS ACCESSORIES!

From: